THE RAPE OF THE AMERICAN
WORKING WOMAN

THE RAPE OF THE AMERICAN WORKING WOMAN

How the Law and the Attitude Violate Your Paycheck

NYLA JO HUBBARD

Algora Publishing
New York

Library of Congress Cataloging-in-Publication Data —

Names: Hubbard, Nyla Jo Jones, author.
Title: The rape of the American working woman: how the law and the
attitude violate your paycheck / Nyla Jo Hubbard.
Description: New York: Algora Publishing, [2016] | Includes bibliographical
    references.
Identifiers: LCCN 2016034488 (print) | LCCN 2016034744 (ebook) | ISBN
    9781628942316 (soft cover: alk. paper) | ISBN 9781628942323 (hard cover:
    alk. paper) | ISBN 9781628942330 (pdf)
Subjects: LCSH: Sex discrimination in employment—Law and legislation—
United States. | Women—Employment—Law and legislation—United States.
| Working class women—Legal status, laws, etc.—United States. | Working
mothers—Legal status, laws, etc.—United States. | Sexual harassment—
Law   and legislation—United States. | Equal pay for equal work—Law and
legislation—United States. | Sex role in the work environment—United States.
Classification: LCC KF3467 .H83 2016 (print) | LCC KF3467 (ebook) | DDC
    331.4/1330973—dc23
LC record available at https://lccn.loc.gov/2016034488

Printed in the United States

Dedicated to My Working Sisters:
May your eyes be opened and
your net pay increased.

TABLE OF CONTENTS

Prologue

This book is not meant to be a criticism of the non-working spouse. I firmly believe that the decision as to whether a woman should work outside the home should be her decision. As a working mother for many years, I am well aware of how difficult it is to work outside the home while also handling house and family. However, many women do not have a choice. They must work to provide for themselves and often for a family. On the other hand, they may choose to work because it contributes additional income, personal satisfaction and provides a service to the outside world. There is no right or wrong choice.

Neither have I intended to voice a complaint about subsidies for the low-income parent. There is no way a mother could be employed making minimum wage, or even well above it, and still meet all the expenses of living and childcare without outside assistance. It is to the betterment of all society that children be properly fed, clothed and educated. We are our brother's (and sister's) keeper.

This book is instead intended to point out the economic disparities that exist under our present system, which greatly benefit the non-working woman and which cost her working sister some of her hard earned pay. The job is already hard; a working woman should not be penalized financially for working (whether by necessity or by choice), a situation which, as I will show in the ensuing pages, is the case.

PREFACE

I do not presume that the observations and advice given in these pages is for everyone. I have used the best data available to me as a layman for my calculations. I am not a professional psychologist, attorney or social worker. What I do have is over forty years of work experience spanning the eras when women began to work in large numbers and the controversy about wages, childcare, sexual harassment and workplace bias really came into play. I offer you the issues. If you find them of interest, I hope you will be part of the solutions.

The ideas behind this book were conceived many years ago, beginning with Mary Ward, my mother, a working woman herself before it was fashionable or even acceptable for women to work. I have been encouraged along the way by many friends and co-workers. The medical technologists, technicians, nurses and aides with whom I worked remain some of my closest friends. It was my experience in the laboratory and the experiences of others that began my quest for justice. You know who you are: Karen, Elaine, Judy, Midge, Ruth, Theresa, Sue, Alicia, Beth, Dolly, Janice, Charlie, Kris, Cherie. I have stood at the bench with all of you and many more. Some of you were there in the bad old days when all the supervisors were men, all the bench techs were women, and the man did not want to hear about it if you had a babysitter problem when he asked you to come in at 4 AM. All of you worked with me and some of you worked for me as I tried, as a manager, to even the score as best I could.

Life teaches us lessons; some are learned the hard way, but even those can be used to educate others. My experience with abuse led me to volunteer at a Domestic Violence shelter and there I drew on the thoughts of other women, some of them advocates for the women at the shelter: Liz, Kim, Katrina, Angel. I owe you so much. I learned also from the clients at the shelter, who cannot be named but who told me how it really is in their lives. You will appear in these pages.

Birders talk when there are no birds to watch, and my work benefitted from old and young birding companions; Carleton, Mary Ella and Loretta, gone but not forgotten; Tracy, advising me from a thousand miles away. One whole chapter would be missing without your suggestions.

I volunteered for a time in a nursing home facility, and the elderly patients did as much for me as I did for them. Even when they can't speak, they can still tell their stories if you listen with your heart. That experience was invaluable when writing the chapter on eldercare.

I learned from my family: my niece and her three children who lived with me for several months after being physically and mentally abused by her husband, and from my daughter, who raised two fine boys and worked throughout the process. I learned from my sister, who did not have it easy but she survives today, a beautiful and active human being. I learned from my brother who made the transition from cared for to caring and does housework as well as yard work without complaint.

Perhaps I would never have put my thoughts to paper if it had not been for my Quaker forebears. You have read the poem *Women's Work* by Moss Rose which appeared in the carefully pasted cuttings of my great-great grandmother Nancy Wilson. Nancy was a Quaker woman with a colorful past, whose family worked in the Underground Railroad after leaving North Carolina for Indiana as the Civil War became imminent. Quakers always believed in educating their girls as well as their boys and many famous reformers were Quakers: Lucretia Mott, abolitionist, Susan B. Anthony, abolitionist/suffragette, Alice Paul, suffragette, Elizabeth Fry, prison reformer and Jessamine West, novelist. Three of these women, Anthony, Mott and Paul, and are so well respected by history that they will soon grace the backs of our $10 bills. Yes, I think they should be on the front, too, but we have to start somewhere.

Susan B. Anthony was alive until shortly before the time that my great great-grandmother saved the poem. The fact that she saved it leads me to believe that Nancy was a supporter of the vote for women. I take sustenance today from the members of my Quaker Meeting, who still follow the Quaker Testimonies of Integrity, Simplicity, Equality and Peace. You are my reservoir of strength.

I also wish to recognize my editor, Andrea Sengstacken, who has patiently coached me through two books. I appreciate your confidence in me, Andrea.

Thank you, Sisters (and some Brothers, too)

Chapter 1. Social Security: The First Rip off

Please, Sister, you need to read this. Yes, I know the dryer just finished and the kitchen is still a mess from dinner, but you need to learn why your paycheck is never quite enough. You are supporting not only yourself and your kids. You are also helping to support a great many women (and some men) who have never worked in their lives. No, I am not talking about Welfare recipients. The Welfare system may well need an overhaul, but at least we can assume that the beneficiaries are needy; and we can hope that, if they aren't really needy, it is considered defrauding the system if they take benefits. I refer to a system where the least needy often benefit the most. I refer to something called Social Security Spousal Benefits, whereby women (and some men) who have not paid one dime into the Social Security system will still receive an amount equal to half of what their spouses receive. Many people mistakenly believe that the spouse is getting half of his. No, this is not one-half of his. It is an additional 50%, which she will receive when she is 62 or older, gratis, simply because the law, as it exists today, favors non-working women.

Dual Entitlement: An example

Cathy's husband, Tom, will receive $2000 per month in Social Security benefits. Cathy has never worked outside the home but she will receive $1000 per month in addition to his benefit so that, as a couple, they will receive $3000 per month, though only Tom paid in. This inequity has developed because in 1935, when Social Security was instituted, Congress realized that, though the benefit at that time might sustain a single person, a couple could not survive on his benefit alone. Congress decided to award a wife an additional sum equal to one half again of his benefit. This was reasonable in 1935 when very few women worked outside the home and benefits were low. However, as more women entered the workforce and more retirees began to receive benefits, it suddenly dawned on Congress that a working woman could be eligible to claim benefits under her own working record and as a spouse under her husband's record as well. To those in power, that would never do. Many of them did not approve of women working outside the home, anyway, so they made sure that working women would sacrifice the benefit they would have received had they stayed home. This is summed up in the "Dual Entitlement Rule."

IRS 00615.020 Dual Entitlement Overview

A. Policy

1. General

A person may be entitled to more than one benefit at the same time. For example, a person may be entitled as a retired worker on his/her own record and as a spouse on another record. However, a person's benefit amount can never exceed the highest single benefit to which that person is entitled. Some benefits are calculated independently with the larger benefit being paid or the smaller benefit being paid plus the excess amount of the larger one. Other types of benefits are calculated with a carry-over reduction amount from the first benefit to the second. (US Social Security Administration, 2015)

What this means, in non-technical language is that a woman is allowed to receive a Social Security benefit either on her own record or on her spouse's record, but not both. Since women make less than men in general, it often happens that the amount that she would have received as a non-working spouse is more than she is entitled to receive on her own earnings record, though she may have worked for decades. In those circumstances, the government generously kicks in the difference of the two, so that she will receive, after paying in for, quite possibly, thirty or forty years, the same amount that she would have received had she never worked a day in her life. She will be drawing on her record but, because she is or was married, in reality she is not benefitting from the Social Security deductions that were taken from her checks. She may have received the same amount by drawing on her husband's record had she never received a paycheck. In that case, the deductions she paid into Social Security all those years are forfeit to the general fund.

I am a sterling example of this inequity as was my mother. She is the one who first informed me of this disparity. Her sister-in-law, who had only worked outside the home for a very short time started receiving her Social Security checks. My mother was gratified to see that Pauline was drawing her benefit as a spouse and it was a tidy sum. My mother believed that she would draw this sum as a spouse in addition to the sum she would draw on her own record after working for thirty or more years. Imagine her chagrin when she discovered that, no, she was not entitled to a spousal benefit though she had raised three children and performed all the same chores as a non-working spouse. She was only entitled to the benefit she earned by working and her contribution as a wife and mother was completely ignored. I am in the same boat. I would receive, should I take "spousal benefits," within a few dollars of the same amount I get for working regularly full-time or part-time for close to forty years. It's enough to make you want to write a book.

You may ask, "What happened to the money my spouse (and other taxpayers) paid in to cover spousal benefit for me if I must draw on my own record and can't take the spousal benefit? " This brings us to the worst aspect of this situation. My deductions (and yours), if you are a married working woman, will wind up helping to pay the benefits of the non-working woman. Since we all pay in at the same rate, 6.2% in 2015 (US Social Security Administration, 2015), the working husband is not paying in a larger sum to cover his non-working wife. She will draw her benefits from the general fund, which you, dear girl, have subsidized.

What I see happening today is that the ones who are cashing in on the spousal benefit are the wealthy women who did not need to work. And just take a look at these statistics. The maximum amount of income susceptible to Social Security taxes is $118,500 in 2015. (Administration U. S., Benefits Planner, Maximum Taxable Earnings 1937-2015, 2015) Many professional or business men make that much. After they reach this level of income, Social Security is no longer deducted, or if it is deducted, it is returned when the taxes are filed. The maximum Social Security paid by any earner, using $118,500 x 6.2% in 2015, is $7,347. If a man pays in the limit, he will receive the highest Social Security benefit — which is $3,501 per month at age 70. (Administration U. S., US Social Security, 2015).

CEO Richard retires at age 70 and gets $3,501 per month from Social Security. His wife, Adele, of the same age, who stayed home to raise a family, is entitled to an additional 50%, so she will receive $1,750.50 every month, though she never paid in one cent. Together they will receive $5,251 per month.

I was a medical technologist for over 30 years, and I have worked at other jobs. Neither I nor any of my co-workers get or will get $1,750.50 per month in our own Social Security, despite the fact that we had to complete a demanding course of study and we all worked horrendous hospital hours, weekends and holidays.

Some might say that a woman is entitled to a benefit since she kept house and often cared for children. I am not denigrating that labor. I've done it, and it is demanding. However, the majority of working women are also keeping house and taking care of children. According to the Pew Research Center, 71% of all mothers work outside the home (Cohn, 2014).

Unlike Adele, divorced mother Crystal comes home to a second job every day. She is obliged to handle the same obligations Adele had: homework, dinner, laundry and bedtime — in less than half the time. Plus, she has already dealt with a day full of stress and her energy is no doubt flagging. Her weekends are taken up with housework, grocery shopping and kid activities because she has no time for those things during the week. She is running on coffee and adrenaline. Yet, if Crystal is making $35,000 per year now, and let's say she is 40 years old and will retire at 65, she will likely get only about $1,789 per month in Social Security benefit twenty-five years from now. She is not eligible for a spousal benefit as she was married less than ten years and it probably wouldn't have benefitted her, anyway.

The truly regrettable side to this situation is the fact that Crystal is also paying Social Security tax on her earnings and will pay it for another 25 years. She is paying for gas to get to work, for clothing appropriate for her job, and for childcare either all day or after school. She pays all this using funds already depleted by her Social Security deductions. And what is her reward? She gets to kick in for Adele's Social Security benefit. She is subsidizing Adele, who gets $1750.50 for which she personally paid nothing and whose husband is already getting $3500 monthly for his benefit alone.

Prior to April 16 of 2016, there was another way to soak the system further called File and Suspend. The husband could file for his benefit at full retirement age but suspend getting his checks at that time. Instead, his wife would start drawing her spousal benefit immediately after he filed (provided she was old enough) and continue to draw her benefit alone until he became age 70 at which time he has, by law, to take his benefit. At age 70, his benefit had increased by 8% per year for the four years he waited. That is, if he applied at age 66 and waited until 70 to get his first check, that check would be 32% higher than it would have been at 66 and his wife would have collected benefits for an extra four years though, once again, she may have paid in nothing (Chatzky, 2015). Thousands of couples used this loophole before it was closed and any couple who filed to suspend before April of 2016 is still using it. (Administration U. S., Recent Social Security Changes, 2015).

An example makes it easier. Doug would file for his Social Security benefit at age 66 which is full retirement age for him. He would be entitled to $2000 per month, but he would suspend his benefit and would not take his checks for the next four years. His wife, Dawn, who worked for less than ten years, still qualified for a spousal benefit of $1000 per month even though he was not drawing. When he turned 70, he would begin taking his payments, but because the benefit increased by 8% for each of the four years he waited, he would get about $2,640 per month at age 70 rather than the $2000. She will still get her $1000 per month. You have helped both of them get more money because she got a benefit without paying in enough to qualify under her own record and having that extra income allowed them to wait until he could get $640 per month more. They should send you a thank you note.

No one is suggesting that we take away great-grandma's Social Security check. (I don't say grandma since I am one myself, and most of the grandmas I know have worked for most of their lives.) Great-grandma is legally entitled to her spousal benefit, as are the women who are qualifying under that rule now. It may not be fair but it is legal. Neither am I saying that a woman should not choose to stay at home (with or without children) if she can and if that is her wish. Of course, she can stay home. She simply won't qualify for Social Security if she doesn't pay in. After all, if her partner is making enough money to support a wife and children during his working years, his resources should be able to cover both of them when he retires. She will not be destitute if he dies first. When her retired husband dies, she will be entitled to either his Social Security benefit or hers. Since his is usually more, she can take his. Dawn will have to give up her $1000 per month spousal benefit, but she will start drawing Doug's $2,640 per month if he dies first. Cathy will get the full $2000 that Tom was getting when he dies (if she was married to him for ten years or more). Adele will get Richard's $3,501 per month. Under the present law, those amounts would still be a loss of income to the wife because she is losing her additional spousal benefit. However, if the law were changed to disallow the spousal Social Security benefit, the widow would still have an income.

One could wonder, if every working woman is obliged to sacrifice the portion of Social Security deductions that would have paid her retirement as a non-working spouse, and working women outnumber non-working women, what happened to the money they paid in and that should have stayed in the system? There should be a surplus. Yet, we all hear about that Social Security is in trouble. Of course, it's in trouble. It is paying benefits to people who are not disabled, who did not pay in and who quite likely don't even need the money. The surplus went to that $1750.50 benefit received by that corporate wife.

If ever a protest was needed, this is the time. Either everyone should have to pay in for the required forty quarters to be eligible for benefits or they should get no benefits. If a corrective law were passed today, there could be a grace period of ten years (forty quarters) or maybe a little more, during which a woman (or a man) could work enough quarters to qualify for benefits. At the end of ten years, everyone would draw on his or her own record, no spousal benefit. If Congress wants to make some provision for non-working spouses, the working spouse should pay in at a high enough rate so as to cover retirement for both parties. This is only fair. Why should your wages cover them?

You may think that there are only a few spouses drawing this unearned benefit but research by the *Tampa Bay Times*, at my request, found that about 7–8% of Social Security retirement benefits go to spouses. That may not sound like a lot but bear in mind that, in 2015, $55 billion was paid in retirement Social Security benefits to retirees (US Social Security Administration, 2015). Seven percent of that figure is $3.71 billion.

And there is a further indignity. A woman (or man) who is divorced after a minimum of ten years of marriage qualifies for spousal benefits. It is not inconceivable that a man who "trades up " in his view, every ten years may leave three or four women drawing on his earnings record though it is just one record. Perhaps none of them worked or they did not work for the full forty quarters. Read this from Tom Margenau, a former Social Security Administration employee, who is in a position to know:

> Q: Can there be more than one woman collecting benefits as a spouse on the same man's Social Security record? In other words, if a man was married twice (or even more) and retires, can his ex-wives get part of his Social Security? And how does that impact the current wife?
>
> A: Yes, more than one woman can receive spousal benefits on the same man's Social Security record. The law says a divorced woman is due benefits on her ex-

husband's Social Security account if she is at least 62, if she isn't due a higher benefit on her own Social Security record, if she was married to the man for 10 years or more, and if she is currently unmarried. Even if she did remarry, benefits would still be due her if that second marriage ended through death or divorce.

The good news for the current spouse is that anything paid to an ex-wife is an add-on supplemental benefit. In other words, payments to the ex-spouse do not offset the current spouse's benefits. And that would be true even if there were more than one ex-spouse. (Margenau, 2009)

Say Richard marries four times and each marriage lasts ten years. You are now subsidizing four corporate wives like Adele at $1,750.50 monthly. That's a figure of $7,002 paid out for them per month, $84,024 yearly, for each year that all four of them live past retirement age. Does your wallet feel thinner?

This bias against the working woman does not stop at retirement benefits. Women who draw on the Social Security record of a spouse (or an ex-spouse of a marriage of ten or more years) for survivor benefits face the same disparity. If a breadwinner dies, the mother of his children will receive benefits for her minor children. However, if she works, her benefits will be reduced should she earn more than $15,720/year in 2015. After that limit is reached, the Social Security administration will take back one dollar for every two dollars that she earns over the $15,720 limit (US Social Security Administration, 2015). This means that, if she earns $25,720/year, she will lose $5000 in benefits. If she does not work, she can receive the entire amount of survivor benefits and probably qualify for food stamps and other subsidies, too. My niece is in this situation. Her ex-husband died. She deals with childcare, transportation of children, and household chores, and she stays on her feet for forty hours a week for $5000 less than she would receive if there was not a penalty on the amount she can earn. She forfeits that $5000 because she is a proud woman who prefers to be a contributing member of society.

I wrote to my senators and representatives about this issue and not one of them even favored me with a reply. It is a political hot potato and the women who would miss out on their "free" benefit have a lot more time to write and call their congressman that you do, with the dryer and the dishes still waiting. Their corporate husbands probably also contribute more to the campaign war chests of said congressional representatives than you do. I realize that you already feel overburdened, but if enough e-mails were sent to senators and congressional representatives and this info was sent to enough newspapers and blogs, politicians would be forced to respond.

Women are unaware of this injustice. This book is an effort to get the word out. We may have to form a coalition. Maybe we can call it Working Women Unite!

Chapter 2. Alimony, Child Support and Divorce Law, Those Who Idled Win

When I divorced in 1990 after twenty-seven years of a difficult marriage, my attorney said to me, "You might have been awarded alimony after such a long marriage. The problem is that you earn $10/hour." I did not want alimony; in fact, I had never considered it, but after hearing that, I decided to research the divorce laws. Once again, ladies, working will not be rewarded.

Alimony is rewarded in different amounts and for different lengths of time depending on the length of the marriage and the age, physical condition and earning capacities of each party.

In Florida, there are three kinds of alimony:

- Bridge the Gap Alimony is designed to help the divorced party adjust to living single and is limited to two years. Bridge the Gap alimony ends upon the death of either party or upon the remarriage of the party receiving alimony.

- Rehabilitative alimony is more extensive and is meant to allow for the training or retraining of a spouse who has not worked. It is for an undefined length of time but there must be a clear plan for the training.

- Permanent Alimony is for life. The idea of alimony is that, if the spouse (usually a wife) has become used to a certain standard of living, the law feels that she should not have to adapt to a less optimal lifestyle due to the divorce. (Statutes of Florida, 2015). Uh, don't divorced working women have to adapt to a lower standard of living?

Did you notice that one of the considerations in granting alimony is the earning capacity of both spouses? If you have been in a long marriage and have never worked, at the present time in Florida you can be awarded alimony for life. However, if you have worked and thereby proven that you are able to support yourself, forget it. You are going to go on working.

A bill was introduced in the Florida Legislature recently that would do away with alimony for life, but it was not signed into law. Alimony is not child support. That is calculated separately and is over and above alimony if alimony is awarded. Alimony is specifically for the financial support of the woman (sometimes men). The theory has been that a woman gives up her career and her earning potential when she marries and stays home to take care of a family. Over time, enough women have suffered after making this choice that it should be obvious that this course of action is unwise. I always told my daughter, "Make sure you are trained in a career for which there is demand and which will allow you to support yourself and any children. Even if you find Prince Charming, he may be unable to work, he could die, or most likely scenario, he could turn out to be a toad in disguise."

The problem with awarding alimony based on the financial resources of each party is that you, working woman, have earned those resources yourself. The non-working women did not. Yet, the average woman who works is going to suffer a sharp decline in her standard of living, too, after a divorce. Her salary, plus child support is not going to add up to the same amount brought in by two working spouses. In addition, in most cases, she will be responsible for getting the kids to school or daycare, meeting with teachers, dealing with doctors' appointments and homework while still holding down a job. The non-working spouse had some part in the decision for her to stay at home and give up her earning potential. If the woman who stayed home deserves extra support, so does the working one who chose not to be dependent.

It is an often proven fact that women suffer a longer lasting financial hit after a divorce. Georgia Dullea was published in *the New York Times*, speaking about divorce, under what was then a new no-fault system: "Her major finding is that, under the new law, a woman's standard of living decreases by an average of 73 percent one year after the divorce while that of her former husband increases by 42 percent." (Dullea, 1985). Other research has found that it is fathers who tend to get richer (Rosen, 2009). Even though he is paying child support, the man of the couple can expect to get raises in pay, his employer will continue to pay into his retirement account and he may marry again and benefit from a new wife's earnings and possessions. His ex-wife has the primary responsibility for the children. Her working hours must be compatible with their hours. It is the rare single mother who can do overtime, business trips and the networking necessary to work her way into the best financial position. Property settlements may appear fair but turn into liabilities. It is often seen as a victory for divorcing women when judges award the home to the wife. However, all too often she cannot keep up with the house costs. The child support plus her income are insufficient to pay the mortgage, so either she winds up losing the home, or she sells it for less than it is worth because she isn't able to hang on and wait for a better price. Claudia Broome, a life coach, corroborates this trend, explaining that when a couple gets divorced, the man's income stays the same or may even increase after a year, while the woman's will have dropped. She explains that the wife, if she has children, often finds herself obliged to turn down offers of advancement at work because of family responsibilities. After four years, she attests, almost 50% of divorced women are still experiencing at least one of several difficulties: late mortgage payments, late or unpaid utility bills, unfilled prescriptions, neglected healthcare, not enough heat, not enough food, no health insurance and the ignominy of going to friends or welfare for help (Broome, 2015).

Making sure you are getting a fair amount of child support over the years is often more than a working mother can keep up with. I worked with a tech who had been married to a doctor and their two sons lived with her. She had worked during his years in medical school, supporting him and their kids. Sometime after he got his MD, he decided he wanted someone else, someone, he probably thought, more befitting to his new position. His ex-wife got child support based on his income as a very newly minted doctor, and I'm sure his student loans were considered as part of his liabilities. In other words, she didn't get much. As the years went by, she considered taking him back to court as his income had multiplied by many times, but the doctor, father of her boys, was wont to poor-mouth. He made sure the boys thought he was strapped for money even though they saw the big house, the boat and the ski vacations. My co-worker knew that if she took him to court, her sons would be led to think she was a gold digger and they would be made to feel that they were a financial burden. She chose to work all her life, coming in at 6 AM and stretching the money while his new trophy wife never worked one day.

There may be reasons for short-term alimony when a woman has small children and no training. There is a policy for such situations in the Florida statutes. However, there should be an additional proviso that she must take courses preparing her for a job which actually has potential. The advice "Do what you love" should be edited to say, "Do what you love that will make you a living." Of course, a fair division of assets is obligatory. If the wife worked to put her husband through school with the idea that he would then share the income while she stayed home to raise their children, and instead he decides he wants to marry his secretary before his career even gets off the ground, she may be entitled to compensation — but for life? I don't think so, unless she is already aged or infirm. Much is dependent on "need" and "ability" as outlined in the previously mentioned statutes. The crux of the matter, to me, is the difference in the way the courts treat working vs. non-working spouses in deciding alimony. The basic tenet is, if you are able to make it yourself, he needn't give you anything. If you chose not to work, you get to go on not working.

You may be wondering why I should include information about alimony in this chapter. You think that you, as the working girl, won't be paying any alimony. First of all, you could be.

If you make the mistake of marrying a man who chooses not to work, and you then divorce him, he can be eligible for alimony. Perhaps, you decided to buy that old Victorian house you had always loved. He tells you that he is handy and can do almost all the work himself. After a few years, you find either he is not making the progress you expected or, worse yet, he is entertaining someone else in that new four-poster bed. He can state that he has not been gainfully employed except in your behalf during the marriage and, even if he was unfaithful, you may live in a no-fault state. The law does not discriminate. You could be paying this colossal disappointment alimony for life and he could even get the house.

On the other hand, imagine if it was your son. He marries a pretty girl (they just will do that, won't they?) whose mother never worked and she decides that she shouldn't have to work, either. She becomes dissatisfied sitting there alone all day while he puts in eighty hours a week providing her with every comfort. She files for divorce. Is she entitled to a lifetime of payments from this hardworking man?

Child Support and Custody: Does Marriage Help?

I watched my friend, Elizabeth, deal with child support or lack thereof for eighteen years. It was painful. It is so easy for some men to hide income and it is so shamefully common for them to do so. My friend, like many of us, did not use the best judgment in choosing her husband but she did choose wisely in her profession. She is a health care professional and has been able to raise two sons on what she makes. That was fortunate because he kicked in only occasionally. She couldn't depend on it and the State of Florida has done a less than stellar job of making sure that he paid his share.

Let's look at the way child support is calculated. There is a handy website for calculating possible support (AllLaw, 2015). We'll start with the support case of John and Cindy. John has a net income of about $65,000 per year. Cindy has not worked outside the home during the marriage. They have two children younger than school age. Cindy will stay in the family home with the children and will receive alimony until the kids are of school age and she has trained for an appropriate job. John will pay the health insurance for the kids of $400 per month. He is also obligated to pay Cindy $1,622/month in child support.

Another couple, Bart and Carol also have two young children but Bart has jumped from job to job. He has no particular training and is now a day laborer, clearing no more than $1000/month. Carol is a medical assistant and brings home about $2000 per month. She will stay in their home, which is rented. She will pay daycare, subsidized, of about $200/month. Medicaid covers the health insurance for the children. Bart is obligated to pay just $50 per month in child support. The judge may try to shame him into working more hours. He may ask why Bart is not able to better support his children; but the sad fact is, if Bart doesn't want to work, no one can make him. If he pays his $50 every month, he has complied with the law. If he doesn't pay it, he may be liable to have his driver's license taken away or even be put in jail (NCSL, 2014). However, Bart can disappear without a lot of effort. Day laborers are very difficult to track.

Now look at Pam and Dave. Dave is a professional and brings home about $6,666/month. The couple has two pre-school children. Pam does not work and she is eligible for alimony. Dave pays the health insurance for the children at $400 per month. Pam puts the kids in a nursery school mornings so she can have some freedom. She pays $600 per month for the daycare. Dave will pay $2,286 per month child support.

Both Jean and Ralph are professionals, both bringing home $6,666 per month. They have two young children. Jean will have the children most of the time and will pay $1,540 in daycare so that she can continue to work. The couple will share the cost of health insurance, each paying $200 per month. Ralph will pay $2,322 per month in child support. Jean is not eligible for alimony.

Do you see the situation here? Jean is working. She has to use a daycare. She is paying half the health insurance and providing the duties of primary caregiver. Yet she will get only $36 per month more child support than Pam will get. Pam chooses to use the daycare on a part-time basis. It is not a necessity. She has none of the expenses of working. It would appear at first glance that Jean's children would have a higher standard of living due to the dual incomes but if you deduct the amount of daycare she is paying and the expenses she incurs by working, all four children will probably have equal benefits. The difference is that Jean is now a single mother. She won't be able to attend daytime functions at the school. She won't be lunching with friends on someone else's money. Once again, where is the justice for the working girl?

Of course, Pam is entitled to child support. However, she would be wise to use that free time and alimony to prepare herself to support those children in the future, should her ex-husband die or lose his job. She may not always get the free lunch.

Of course, being awarded child support and actually receiving it are two very different things. Professionals probably have bank accounts and tax returns. Fathers who work for themselves or on sales commissions are far more likely to dissemble. Even if the father can be found, and some income proven, the father is allowed a lot of leeway before punitive measures take hold. If he is thousands of dollars behind, the court will give him a period of time to pay. Too often, he pays just enough to get under the maximum amount, the amount that triggers action by child support collection authorities. If he makes a couple of payments, he is now under the maximum limit and he falls off the radar. The authorities will not look for him again until he is once again over the limit. At that time, a new case will commence. He can play this game for eighteen years. He will be behind and still be liable for child support after the kids are of age but the mother needs it while they are growing up.

Do not get the idea that the father will not be able to see his kids per agreement, even though he does not pay child support. One has no effect on the other, at least not in the state of Florida. The mother is not allowed to keep the children from him if the divorce agreement gives him a right to see them. Of course, they are his children and they may want to see their father but it must be galling for a mom who works every day and struggles to cover the cost of housing, food, clothing and all the other expense to watch them go off happily with someone who is not facing up to his responsibility. She can only hope that he will buy them a Happy Meal.

Another legal mess for women, and this time it isn't just the working ones, is the issue of custody. Our lawyers will tell you that Florida does not have custody. In Florida, both parents have "time sharing" with their children (Cordell, 2016). There is no primary or secondary custody. Child support paid by either parent will depend on how much time the child spends with that parent. Only overnights are used to calculate the percentage of time-shared.

Time-sharing is a double-edged sword. My friend's ex did not bother much with his children (or with his child support) until he remarried and had three more children. My friend loved having the kids to herself since he seldom bothered to see them. At the same time, however, she knew the boys were hurt by his lack of attention. Then, suddenly he started taking them every other weekend. By this time, they had three little half-brothers to watch while Mom and Dad went out to dinner. The older ones served as free baby sitting.

This is the situation when kids are shared between previously married parents. It is not the case with unmarried parents. I first became aware of the difference in parental rights between unmarried parents while working at a domestic violence shelter.

If a mother is not married to the father of her child, and especially if she has not named him on the birth certificate, she need not share that child with him. The natural mother is presumed to have primary custody of that child unless she can be proven unfit. If the father wants any time-sharing with the child, he must prove paternity and must win visitation rights (Clarke, 2016). Of course, if she wants child support from the father, the mother will have to be willing to share the child, but many of the women I have met in the shelter know that they won't be able to count on the money. If they try to get it, he will then be eligible for time with the kids and he will therefore always know where the mother is. If they are in shelter, they are trying to escape him. Thus they often choose, instead, to work all their lives at whatever job they can find — and he gets off scot-free.

We hear, on the news, about how marriage is falling out of favor, about the "decline of morality." All I can say is, under the present law, divorced women with abusive husbands would have been better off if they had never married the children's father. They would not have to share the kids. He would not be around to be a bad influence and the mom most likely winds up not getting the money to which she was entitled by virtue of marriage anyway. Maybe, it is the law that should fall out of favor.

Adequate child support is a must, and a fair property settlement, likewise. But giving alimony for life to a woman who didn't choose to support herself makes women in general look like a lazy bunch of moochers. And "us working girls" are not mooching!

CHAPTER 3. HAVE WE REALLY COME A LONG WAY,
BABY? A SHORT HISTORY OF WOMEN'S WORK IN AMERICA

Women have always worked. The remains of Native American women from the Southwest have been found along with the pottery they made and the matate they used to grind their corn. Eskimo women traditionally used their teeth to soften the seal skins they made into clothes. The women of the Afar tribe with whom I worked in Ethiopia did all the heavy work. They made their houses by bending limber branches and covering them with mats, which they wove themselves from rushes they gathered at the river. Of course, all these women also cooked and cared for the children and kept life organized. In early times, these endeavors were recognized as the necessities they were; but now, we don't have to chew seal skins or build our own houses, and the routine work of keeping a suburban house clean and the laundry done can go unappreciated and provides little sense of reward.

In the early nineteenth century, before the Industrial Revolution, most men as well as women worked at home. In their book *America's Working Women*, the editors point out that at that time, even when women brought in extra income by taking in boarders or by sewing or doing outside laundry, they still didn't get much credit. That work was simply considered further domestic chores, and the family income was still attributed strictly to the man of the house, even when his income alone could not have covered the expenses of the household (Baxandall, Rosalyn and Gordon, Linda, 1995).

At that time, if women went out to work, it was most often "in service," being maids, nannies or cooks. Many came to this country as indentured servants when there were not enough resources in their home countries; they worked the prescribed seven years in their new country to earn their independence. After they finished their indenture, most probably hoped to marry as there wasn't much opportunity otherwise, and most women wanted (and still want) families. Among those who still needed to support themselves, some worked in or were the proprietors of taverns. There were also seamstresses, though it is doubtful that they made anything close to the income of a male tailor.

Having maids in households inevitably led to liaisons, either with or without consent, and there are many records of an extension of indenture time levied on an indentured female servant if she gave birth to a child while under indenture — often as long as a year of additional service (Records of Anne Arundel Court, 1703-1765). If the child she bore belonged to her master, she still had to work out her indenture time per Virginia statute, and some masters tried to get the woman's time extended for the crime of bearing his own child (Baxandall, Rosalyn and Gordon, Linda, 1995). Then, as now, the law was not a working girl's best friend.

The era of the 1800s encompassed the move west. Having read numerous accounts of pioneer women, cooking, washing and having babies on the Trail or in sod houses, I am led to believe that it was probably not the first choice of many these women to go West. It is far more likely that they were forced to do so by circumstances. As the East filled up, there was often no affordable land to be had in their home states. Oldest sons frequently inherited the family farm and younger brothers were expected to either help out or find a place of their own somewhere else. There was also the quest for religious freedom, as in my own family. My father's people had settled in North Carolina, but Quakers with their stand on abolition were not welcome in slave states. In many Quaker families at the time, Dad, Mom and the kids all loaded up and fled to the Midwest.

I am sure in many cases of pioneer resettlement, the husbands were entranced by stories of good fortune heard fourth or fifth hand from itinerant salesmen or travelers and, overnight, the family was heaved out of whatever comfort they had and set on the trail to a new life. I can just imagine the angst those young wives must have felt in leaving everything and everyone behind and the isolation they suffered on far-flung ranches and homesteads miles from any other family, no radio, no television and certainly no internet to link them to the outside world.

The sewing machine was invented in the nineteenth century and women began to work in boot making and textile mills. Pictures tell the story on the website of the national Women's History Museum of women crammed together in a textile mill working on open machinery. In Philadelphia in the 1930s, 64% of the female mill workers were newcomers either from other countries or from the countryside. Women made an average of $2.25 per week compared to men's earnings of $6.50–$7. This disparity, along with poor working conditions, led to women's involvement in labor organizations. In 1834 a strike was staged that, though largely unsuccessful, began the process that culminated with the formation of the Lowell Female Labor Reform Association (National Women's History Museum, 2007). It was necessary for women to form their own unions as men often resisted having women in the membership of their own trade unions though they worked in the same industry or even in the same factory (Baxandall, Rosalyn and Gordon, Linda, 1995).

The Civil War saw the influx of women into nursing as a career, and other fields as well. Many women were left without husbands after the war, and they entered the work force by necessity. The first large scale national labor union was formed in 1869, titled The Knights of Labor. In 1881, the Knights voted to include women.

In the latter half of the nineteenth century, there were efforts to improve the lot of women in the garment trades. Susan B. Anthony tried to get women to take the jobs of striking printers, but this only angered the striking men. The suffragists and the women's rights movement at the time were not as helpful to female factory or domestic workers as they might have been. The causes the movement focused on were relevant to the times, as they tried to take on wife beating, birth control, divorce and equal pay; but the suffragettes and reformers were mostly well off gentry and they failed to notice the women in their own households, the ones doing the laundry, cooking, minding the children and making their garments (Baxandall, Rosalyn and Gordon, Linda, 1995). One wonders if it wasn't just too inconvenient to have their own help asking for better pay.

The turn of the century saw a massive expansion of manufacturing and clerical jobs. Though women still made up only 20% of the burgeoning middle class in 1920, more and more women were working outside the home and finding satisfaction in their work, even though the hours were long and the pay low. Women were often glad to escape the drudgery of the kitchen and the field and to have money of their own or to use for helping their families. The American Federation of Labor, the AFL, was formed during this time, largely replacing the Knights of Labor. The first president of the AFL shared the prevailing sentiment that women should remain in the home; women did not find the support they needed under his leadership. This led some of them to join the Women's Trade Union League, the WTUL. In 1909, female seamstresses in shirtwaist factories staged a strike after being dismissed for union activity. The activity was in response to overcrowded factories without proper fire escapes. One banner read, "We are starving while we work; we might as well starve while we strike." Labor leaders settled, though the factory owners still did not implement safety measures and it took the huge fire at the Triangle Shirtwaist Factory in 1911, resulting in 146 deaths, to prod the passage of more stringent laws to protect workers (Leckie).

This country has passed multiple laws to assure fair compensation. Beginning with the New Deal in 1938, efforts were made to force employers to pay a living wage. Using the Fair Labor Standards Act, FLSA, Franklin D. Roosevelt wanted to make the minimum wage 25¢ per hour and to limit the work week to 40 hours. The law also assured overtime pay if a worker put in more than the stated number of hours in a week. When the law reached Congress, Southern politicians objected because field hands, household workers and others, if paid the required wage, would undermine the profit of their employers. In order to get the bill passed, Roosevelt gave in to their demands and the most vulnerable of workers, many of them women, were left out of the sweeping reform that lifted many others out of poverty (Grossman, 1978).

According to Caroline Frederickson, there was general resistance to women taking any of the jobs provided by the New Deal. There was much written in the press criticizing women who wanted to work. Writer Frank Hopkins asked, "Would we not all be happier if we could return to the philosophy of my grandmother's day, when the average woman took it for granted that she must content herself with the best lot provided by her husband?" (Frederickson, 2015) Of course, this ignored the women who did not have husbands or, for whatever reason, their husbands did not work. Some states had laws excluding women from state jobs; and many school districts would not hire women who were married — or they fired the existing teacher if she did marry (Frederickson, 2015).

While the plight of the female factory worker is well documented, the work of the women on the farm went on with no fanfare from early morning often until late at night. My own grandmothers were responsible for getting the breakfast ready at dawn, while the milking was done; no cereal and milk here, but rather eggs, ham, gravy, homemade bread or biscuit and plenty of it. After the kitchen was cleaned, the milk had to be processed: cream separated, butter churned and all stored in a cool place. By mid-morning, the chickens were fed, slow layers identified and their heads chopped off. The hot work of scalding, plucking and butchering ensued and preparations were made for dinner, as the noon meal was the largest of the day. Lots of peeling and chopping went on as masses of mashed potatoes were served with melting butter nestled in a crater at the top. I remember helping Grandma when I was no more than four years old. I would transfer the mashed potatoes from the pan to the serving dish and Grandma would encourage me to "mound it up, Jody. Make it look like it's plenty." All the food had to be ready when the men broke for their meal, and the farmwife's reputation as well as that of her husband depended on how good the food was and how timely was the service.

After again cleaning up the kitchen, Grandma went outside. The garden was either planted, watered, hoed, picked or all of the above. In summer, the peas had to be shelled before they were cooked or canned, the corn cut off the cob, tomatoes prepared for canning and the canning done. Of course, time had to be found to keep up a thirteen-room house and, in the case of my mother's mother, eleven children had to be birthed, fed, clothed and kept out of trouble. The work never stopped and this was in my lifetime. Is it any wonder that my own mother went to work in a factory at the first opportunity?

Let's go back to the eleven children. Margaret Sanger, a nurse by training, worked to bring birth control to the country's women after seeing her own mother weakened by the births of eleven children and eighteen pregnancies. She felt that there could be no freedom, no self-determination for women, particularly the poor, so long as they had baby after baby, far beyond their ability to feed them or the physical strength to care for them. After finding herself caring for women who had been reduced, by necessity, to illegal abortions, she began her work in contraception. She coined the term birth control and provided diaphragms to women as well as information. She founded the American Birth Control League, the precursor to the Planned Parenthood Federation in 1921. It was an uphill battle. In 1914, Sanger risked jail when she sent out information, just information, on contraception. The Comstock Act of 1873, passed ostensibly to prohibit obscene material, included (by design) the prohibition on giving out any information and/or devices intended for contraception. Sanger went to England to avoid arrest but was later jailed for opening and operating the first birth control clinic in the US in 1916. It was not until the late 1930s that birth control was finally made legal in the United States and then only upon the prescription of a doctor. Sanger lived to see the birth control pill become available and probably thought the war was won (Biography. com staff, na). Yet today, one hundred years after the first birth control clinic opened, women are still struggling to be informed about pregnancy prevention and still must fight for access to free or low-cost birth control, while babies are born by the thousands to mothers who hadn't planned on having children at that time and have no resources to provide for them. There have been repeated efforts in our Congress to deprive Planned Parenthood of funding, primarily by Republican congressional representatives (though some of the founding mothers and fathers of Planned Parenthood were, in fact, Republicans). According to Cecile Richards, president of Planned Parenthood, the recent Republican led Congress voted to end the National Family Planning Program that was started by Richard Nixon, a Republican president. This action flies in the face of recent reductions in teen pregnancy, a thirty-year low in America, due to better sex education and access to birth control (Smith, 2016). Planned Parenthood provides more than birth control. Many women rely on the Planned Parenthood clinics for gynecological health care. Where will they go if the clinics are shut down? Margaret Sanger must be spinning in her grave.

By the 1940s, for a stay at home mom, traditional housework became a lonely occupation since each woman was doing it in her own house. There were few communal work efforts like the old quilting bee or chatting at a barn raising. After the children reached school age, the bored housewife must have found it tempting to join the workforce. Centuries of conditioning die hard, however. Women were still used to being told what to do, so even when they took a job they expected to take a submissive place in the working order. I remember my Great-aunt, who became a nurse in about 1920, telling me that, as a unit, the nurses were expected to stand up when a doctor entered the room! With this sort of class-consciousness, it is not surprising that women's wages still did not keep with those of men, even when they were doing the same thing.

Women also had a hard time getting working conditions improved. Baxandall and Gordon give an example of a meat packer in 1934. She and her co-workers had to handle the meat when it was hot and steaming. In the summer, women were known to pass out from the overwhelming heat. There were no guards on the machine used to make hot dogs. One of the women got her fingers caught and lost them to the machine. A few of the women organized a work stoppage resulting in the provision of safety devices on the machines, but the company discovered which of the women were involved in the protest and they were fired. Even when the New Deal, purported to be the savior of the working man, became law, it didn't include women. Perhaps it was meant to be inclusive at the federal level, but local bosses excluded women from the work programs.

Finally, in 1933 President Roosevelt asked Frances Perkins to be his Secretary of Labor. She reported that she would only take the job if she could do something about the long hours and poor pay, particularly of children. The first minimum wage law was passed. It did away with most child labor and it did include women workers (Grossman, 1978). Still, there was general prejudice against married women working. It was a struggle for those wives who needed or wanted to work. They persevered and their numbers kept rising. In 1920, married women made up 23% of the labor force. By 1940, the percentage was 36%, and the war years saw the number soar (Baxandall, Rosalyn and Gordon, Linda, 1995).

During World War II, 310,000 women worked in the US aircraft industry alone and women were actively recruited. Remember Rosie the Riveter. Women were vital to the war effort. Nevertheless, despite the need for the labor of women, they were still expected to work for less, often earning 50% less than the men (History.com staff, 2010). The ability to pay women less increased profits for the corporations and, had the women even considered striking, patriotism in a time of war would have been a great deterrent.

Nor was there parity for women in uniform. Three hundred fifty thousand women served in the US Armed Forces during World War II both abroad and at home. One hundred thousand WACs served and there were thousands of female officers. The women's Air Force Service Pilots provided services ferrying planes and participating in training missions (History.com staff, 2010). Yet just yesterday a story appeared in the *Tampa Bay Times*, about 95-year-old Elaine Harmon of Silver Spring, MD, who was a "WASP," a Women Airforce Service Pilot. Elaine died in April, having requested that her ashes be buried in Arlington National Cemetery. Her request was denied. The Army has ruled that her unit was not technically part of the military. The irony is that if Elaine had been married to a veteran, though she never served one day in the military herself, she would be accepted in Arlington with no problem (*The New York Times* staff, 2016).

After World War II ended, most of the women employed during the war wanted and expected to keep working, including the married women. However, the men needed jobs when they came home, and women found themselves shunted aside to make room. There were those who fought back and there were employers who wanted to keep their experienced help, so the percentage of women working in industry and finance never returned to pre-war levels. Society was slow to accept this new norm and President Truman himself blamed juvenile delinquency on mothers not being at home (Baxandall, Rosalyn and Gordon, Linda, 1995). I have heard the same sentiment from older adults today, but I am old enough to know many adult children of both working and non-working mothers and I believe that the children of working mothers often turn out to be more can-do people than are the offspring of mothers who did for them.

The Women's Movement

Though women had been campaigning for equal rights and privileges since the time of Lucy Stanton and Susan B. Anthony, there came a lull after women finally got the right to vote in 1920. The flapper era was a reaction to the long time constraints on women, coupled with the general exuberance of the Roaring Twenties that expressed relief at the end of the First World War. It might have been followed by legal reforms and further advances, if not for the Depression that followed. The country had too many other problems at that time for the rights of women to be a priority.

By the outbreak of the Second World War, women were again, or still, trying to be heard. The cartoon character of Wonder Woman, conceived in 1941, was supposed to be a vehicle for espousing women's rights. She was depicted as an Amazon, female to the core but so strong that she was able to break her bonds in practically every comic strip (Lepore, 2014). Men as well as women loved Wonder Woman. Unfortunately, they appeared not to connect the bondage of their heroine with the real life bondage of many, indeed most, of the women around them.

I was 25 in 1970, exactly the right age to identify with "women's liberation" when it became a movement again. I had been primed by a mother who was a libber before "libbing" had a name. She was incensed when the birth of Princess Caroline of Monaco was celebrated with only a 21-gun salute while Prince Albert, the male child, got 101. Years later, she was further incensed when she found out she was not going to get her spousal benefit from Social Security because she had worked outside the home..

As for myself, I was first married to a retrograde-thinking man from a retrograde-thinking family; and my mother-in-law, who was a strong woman herself, thought the man should discuss decisions with his wife but the final decision should always be his. With some men this might have worked, if they were willing to listen and consider, but many men didn't bother. No doubt they thought, "If I'm going to get my way, anyhow, why discuss it?"

In the clinical laboratory where I began work in 1968, it was rare to find a female supervisor. The laboratory heads were almost invariably male and the techs were all female. There was precious little "discussion" in the lab or at home. If the supervisor decided you should come in at 4 AM, it was up to the tech to make that happen. Meanwhile, I had a two-year-old child, as several of us did, and the day care center did not open until 7 AM. The pay was abysmal but we all accepted it, because we wanted to do what we were trained to do. In the evenings, though, we saw the news and the protests and we identified with the words of the movement leaders, as we knew our own worth whether the supervisors did or not.

It was during the women's movement that women started to become police officers, park rangers, mail carriers and all manner of new titles. We now take these things for granted but it was an uphill battle every day for those female pioneers. The movement was not just about jobs. Leaders called for reproductive rights, easier access to contraceptives and abortion. Access to education was a big item as women in increasing numbers wanted to enter medical and law school and women's sports benefitted when Title IX finally made it mandatory for schools to fund and sponsor all girl teams (Burkett, 2016).

Though it took close to twenty years, the pay scale in the lab finally began to reflect our skill and training and to be evenly apportioned between male and female techs. I believe the reason for the change was the growth of Florida. We had so many Medicare patients that hospitals were desperate for techs. They had to pay. Other occupations have not come so far and the pay of men and women is still not equal, as you will see in the next chapter.

It took far longer than twenty years for women to be recognized in the area of inventions. In her book *Rain: a Natural and Cultural History*, author Cynthia Barnett tells the story of Mary Anderson who invented the windshield wiper and patented it in 1903. The auto industry scoffed at her device and told her it was not practical. Yet, windshield wipers were standard equipment by 1913 (Barnett, 2015). A woman, Elizabeth Magie, invented the forerunner of the "Monopoly" game. She was making a social statement with her game, which she called "The Landlord's Game," as a protest against the robber barons of her time. She filed a legal claim for the game in 1903 but Charles Darrow renamed the game and, claiming it as his own, sold it to Parker Brothers. Darrow made millions. Magie complained and was finally given all of $500 as a settlement (Pilon, 2015).

While studying for my degree, I remember reading about Rosalind Franklin who used x-ray diffraction to demonstrate the structure of DNA. Her photograph was shown to Watson and Crick without her knowledge. Watson and Crick were able, by using her photograph, to discern the double helix and go on to receive a Nobel Prize. She did not receive credit for many years and died before seeing Watson and Crick receive the prize.

Some of these women were British but the attitude existed on both sides of the Atlantic. We would like to think that things have changed now, and it is indeed more common to see recognition of women scientists and inventors, but Laura Hoopes of Pomona College in California warns us that women can become complacent and not realize that the old attitudes are still out there until "it hits them in the face" (Lee, 2013).

I hope that the younger generation of men will demonstrate less of "the attitude." It is certainly alive and well in my generation. I live in a condo community. There is little point in any woman making a request to our Board, the majority of board members being elderly men who have "made it" financially — if not cerebrally. Perhaps, if the woman was young and pretty, there might be some hope, but the answer to me and any other woman having the temerity to speak up has always been "no," even when the same request has been granted for other home-owners. When I complained that their response was discrimina-tory, one of them asked my husband, "Can't you control her?" Is it any wonder why so many women are angry?

Nevertheless, we have made progress. One area that has shown great improvement is the ability to get credit. Strange as it may seem to younger women, in the 1960s it was impossible for a women to get credit without documenting the income and signature of a parent or husband as guarantor. Legislation in that decade made it possible for a woman to buy a car or a house on credit under her own record, and further laws, including the Equal Credit Opportunity Act, aimed to stop lenders from using race or gender when deciding whether to grant loans (NFCC staff, 2016). At least it made it harder for them to do so.

We have made great strides, most of which we owe to brave women who came before us. Isaac Newton said "If I have seen fur-ther than others, it is by standing upon the shoulders of giants." That is certainly true of progress for women. Yet, it is still not easy for a woman to work and to receive commensurate pay, nor is it easy for a woman to be in business for herself. It is, no doubt, dif-ficult for a man to open his own business, too, but read the follow-ing statistics. The *Huffington Post* reports that women received only seven percent of venture capital funds in 2013 — and not because there were few women asking for the loans. Research indicated that investors were simply more likely to lend money to a man than to a woman, even though the proposal was the same. We still think of entrepreneurs as men (Brinegar, 2016).

Linda Stevenson, senior vice-president of National City Bank and Director of its Women's Business Development Program, does not agree that it is more difficult for women to get loans for the purpose of starting a business. She says that the primary problem is that women are less likely to ask for loans, preferring instead to use their own money because they hesitate to take on debt. She believes that women could profit from the option of using other people's money and banks should be willing to loan them that money because women pay their bills (Wilmerding, 2006).

Risk-averse women and risk-averse bankers aren't likely to make a good partnership. Bankers think in dollar signs and so must women in start-ups. Even though Ms. Stevenson may feel that part of the blame for the lack of money loaned to women for investment rests in the timidity of women, she has done what she can to make loans more available for women, heading up a program to lend more to women-owned businesses (Wilmerding, 2006). She must think there is a need for a hand-up.

The Small Business Administration has a branch called the Office of Women's Business Ownership whose mission statement is to "enable and empower women entrepreneurs (US Small Business Administration, 2016). The National Business Women's Council states that women received only two percent of total funding from outside equity compared to eighteen percent for men. Growth potential was directly proportional to the dollar amount of external equity used (Business Women's Council, 2012). Women must insist on equal opportunity to funding for their businesses.

It is also recommended that women look to sources other than banks for their business investment loans. Local government programs may be available for investment in the community and there are micro loan entities such as Count-Me-In for Women's Independence who offer smaller loans as well as education and counseling (Wilmerding, 2006).

Yes, there can be roadblocks to women who want to go into business for themselves, but other women and government entities are making an effort to help you to work for yourself. Moreover, don't discount the idea of enrolling a partner. We all know of partnerships that have gone sour, but they can also work; and a partnership spreads the risk and the heavy decision-making as well as the profit. Women have been co-operating since the beginning of time in order to survive in a world run by men.

When I was in Paris, being prepped for my mission with MSF (Doctors without Borders) in Ethiopia, the advisor said to me, "Your team will sustain you." She meant that I would be a long way from home, in an entirely differently culture, the only American. She knew there would be times when I felt lonely and adrift. She could only help me so much with her advice on not using hand gestures and not insulting my host country. She was telling me to rely on my team. I will tell you to rely on your team. Not only did my team sustain me in Ethiopia, but the Afar women of the tribe whom we treated also sustained me. They had a sisterhood I could only envy. They had few rights and suffered great injustice but they had each other. They reached out to me, though I was white and they didn't speak a word of English. They stopped at the lab and looked at the photos of my family. They introduced their children. They provided me with a stool to sit on and some porridge to eat. You will find sisters to sustain you. Judge well, as every woman you meet won't be sister material, but our sisters have worked for us through many ages, and it is our turn to work with and for them.

Chapter 4. The Gender Biased Pay Scale

Actress Patricia Arquette wrote what the *Tampa Bay Times* called "an impassioned plea for equal pay...backed by eye-popping data." Ms. Arquette states that the inequality in earnings between a man and woman over a lifetime amounts to two houses, 14 cars and 37 years of family meals." (DePillis, 2015)

In US dollars, that is $431,360. The median yearly income for a full-time American working man is $47,415, while the median American working woman makes just $36,931, a difference of $10,784. These are figures averaged over a forty-year work life.

The situation has certainly not improved since the recent recession and the subsequent partial recovery. The *Washington Post* ran an article showing how wages have been impacted since the comeback. Their research showed that mid wage jobs, those paying between $13.83 and $21.13 per hour, made up about 60% of the jobs lost, and only 27% of jobs available now are in that range. Further, they found that jobs that pay less $13.83 per hour have "utterly dominated" the so-called recovery, making up 58% of the gain since 2010. The *Post* reports that this data came from an earlier report from the National Employment Law Project (Plumer, 2013)

So what kinds of jobs are we talking about, that so many people perform for low wages? About 40% of the jobs made available during this economic cycle include food service, retail and a broad category including sales and office clerks (Plumer, 2013). What gender do you suppose is doing most of these jobs? That's right, your working sisters. Sixty-six percent of the low-wage work force was female two years ago (Business Women's Council, 2012).

Food service jobs are often tipped positions. By federal standards, a tipped employee is one who gets more than $30 per month in tips. This rule allows workers who only get an occasional tip to be excluded from the tip law. But there is much to understand about the laws regarding tipped employees. First, a specific minimum wage applies to wait staff and others who rely on tips. The federal requirement for minimum wage for tipped workers is $2.13 and has been $2.13 for 23 years. State law varies widely. In Florida, the minimum cash wage is $5.03. Employers in Florida can use tip income to make up the difference between the $5.03 and the state stipulated combined cash and tip wage of $8.05. The combined cash-and-tip wage in some states is lower, as low as the federally mandated wage of $7.25. Some states require employers to pay the standard minimum wage or above, regardless of whether the employee gets tips (Labor U. D., Wage and hour division, 2016). All tips are supposed to be reported for income tax purposes by the tenth of the month following the month during which the tips were received. The employer must withhold both Social Security and Medicare tax from the tip total as well as income tax. The IRS tells the employers of tipped personnel that the total tip income reported to them must equal at least 8% of the gross total receipts of the restaurant, so restaurants have an incentive to insist that their wait staff report tips (IRS, Small Business and Self Employed, 2015).

When a tip is included on a credit card, there is a record of the tip and this helps ensure reporting; but the employer is allowed to withhold from the tip the percentage that the credit card company will charge the restaurant for accepting the card. Credit card charges vary from 2% up to 5%. So, if you tip the waitress $10 and the credit card company charges 3%, the restaurant will withhold 30 cents from that tip. It doesn't sound like much, but over a month's time, it adds up.

There is also a practice of tip pooling. In many restaurants, all the people involved in serving the customer pool their tips and the tips are then disbursed according to how much time the particular person spent with the customer. This means that, if an employee only brings the bread, he won't get as much of the tip as the person who takes the order, delivers the drinks, etc. A pool arrangement is only legal if all staff members agree to the arrangement (US Dept.. of Labor, 2016).

There have been instances where wait staff were cheated of tip income because supervisory personnel or others were included in the pool. Tipped workers in general have less control of their wages because it is impossible to know in advance what one will receive in tips. Women are particularly affected by this, as women make up two-thirds of tipped workers nationally. Jobs depending on tips are common among poor women, and poverty is twice as frequent among tipped workers as among workers overall.

Women in states that pay tipped workers standard minimum wage regardless of tips are far less likely to be poor. Even among those states, women make only 80 cents compared to the one dollar earned by men among tipped workers. In other states, they make less (Katherine Gallagher Robbins, 2014). It seems reasonable to me that due to family responsibilities women, particularly mothers, may be less able to take the dinner and late evening shifts that no doubt pay the best in tips. Regular daycares are not open in the evening, subsidized daycare included.

Education helps lift women up from the low wage quagmire, but not as much as it should. It is discouraging to learn that the pay gap is not closing for the youngest college graduates. Last year female college grads were making 84% of what the just-graduated male workers were making. This year the women are making only 79%. The Economic Policy Institute gives the reason for this drop as a rise in wages for the men and a decrease for women. The study looked into the old excuse that the gap was because women take time off for having and raising children, but this latest study found that the gap begins long before women are even thinking about maternity leaves. Men are simply paid an average of $9,000 more per annum from the first year they start working after college. This is partly due to the type of work they chose, as the top fields for men were: software developer, computer systems administrator and construction project manager. For women the top fields were: elementary school teacher, registered nurse, and human resources specialist.

The male occupations paid more at a starting average of $40,800 per year while the female jobs paid on average $31,090 yearly to start (*The Washington Post* staff, 2016). We could argue that teaching and nursing are certainly as valuable as writing software and heading up a company's IT department, but the market determines what those occupations will make and since women will do them for less money, the wages stay low.

The next question is whether the gap remains when men and women do the same jobs. Research has found that, when the same job is considered, men still make more. The smallest disparity is often in the lowest paying jobs. Food preparation and serving showed little difference in pay between men and women. The numbers begin to climb with office work and spike with financial advisors and managers, sales, production supervisors and physicians and surgeons. Yes, though 37% of all doctors are women, male doctors make $756 more per week than female doctors make. Male surgeons make 37.76% more than female surgeons. Male CEOs, making up 70% of all CEOs in the US, make a median amount of $674 more per week that their female counterparts. With financial managers and advisors, the difference is between $544 and $633 per week. In only one job studied was the wage the same, and that job is medical support technologist and technician, the job I held for many years. I have already told you that this equality was a long time coming (Baxter, 2015).

Because of the secrecy with which companies treat salary information, it is usually impossible to know exactly what a co-worker is making. At the hospital consortium where I worked, it was grounds for dismissal to discuss your salary with another worker. However, a study done by Phillip N. Cohen and Matt L. Huffman of the University of North Carolina at Chapel Hill queried the 2000 census data and found that women on average made only 81% of what men made for the same job. That study was based on 30,000 job classifications and involved 1.3

million workers. Only a few are able to break the "glass ceiling" and achieve parity in senior management. Even then, the number of women in moderate to upper management has dropped by 13% in the past decade from 32% in 1990 to 19% in 2000 (Kennedy, 2010).

Disparity exists among winnings between male and female athletes. In March of this year, five top female soccer players filed suit against US Soccer, demanding equal pay for equal work. The US Women's National Team, USWNT, has won three World Cups since 1992 while the US Men's National Team, USMNT, has won none. Yet, female soccer players contend that they earn up to 40% less despite their prowess. Hope Solo, one of the complainants, says, "We are the best in the world. We have three World Cup championships and four Olympic Championships." Ms. Solo goes on to say of the male players, "they get more to show up than we get to win major championships" (Das, 2016).

The reason usually given for the fact that female athletes are being paid less is that they do not draw the same size crowds, but the Women's World Cup in July of 2015 was the most-watched soccer game ever in the US.

Tennis involving both genders is well attended both in person and on television. Tennis, unlike soccer, is the most gender equitable of all the sports (Walters, 2016). Conversely, golf, though millions of women play the game, has widely divergent payment for winning. The Ladies Professional Golf Association, LPGA, was formed in 1950 due to sparse tournaments and small winnings. That group has made improvements but parity in purses between the Men's and the Women's Opens has been slow to occur. Two years ago, both men and women played golf on the same course. Yet Martin Kaymer won $1.62 million for his victory at the US Men's Open while Michelle Wie won only $320,000 for her win in the Women's Open. The United States Golf Association, the USGA, treats men and women equally as amateurs but the gap widens when they go professional. The USGA reported revenue of $103 million from its 2014 tournaments. Many women are calling for golf to follow tennis in equal pay for equal skill (Saffer, 2016).

Recently a friend told me that her sister, who is an interim pastor, was much in demand by churches where she interviewed. The reverend was told by several churches that they preferred a female pastor. The church elders mentioned easier approachability, more empathy, a less patriarchal attitude. I'm sure all that is true and I know this woman to be a good pastor but, when I researched the subject, I found another reason why churches might prefer women. They cost less. In a compensation study conducted by Church Law and Tax Report, there was a pay gap of $10,000 between male and female pastors. When various positions within the ministry were compared, there was a gap of as much as $25,000.

When asked about salary requirements, some women were so eager to work in the field that they would take a job regardless of a low salary. Female pastors sometimes were a secondary breadwinner and felt that they could do with less. The problem with adopting this approach is that it lowers the bar for those who come after you. It allows the hiring group to set a lower salary for applicants in the future, who might find it hard to live on the amount offered; and it gives the impression, in general, that women will take less than they are worth (Moon, 2014). Since the number of women in traditional seminaries is now about equal with men, this is not a good tradition to begin. More women attend church regularly than do men so you, as female clergy, will be ministering to your own sisters (Piatt, 2014). It seems that they would want you to be paid fairly.

One of the few places where men and women are paid equally is in the military. Since every job is graded and the wage for each pay grade is published, there is no way the different sexes can be paid differently for the same job. In the past, women have not been promoted at the same rate as men, but that was partly because not all jobs were open to women in the military. Between 1993, when women were allowed to serve on ships and squadrons, and 2015, more women have reached the higher ranks. There were no female generals in the military in 1993. In 2015, there are 38 female generals, 7.9% of the total number (Schrager, 2015). Last year, it was announced by Secretary of Defense Ashton Carter that he intended for all positions in the military to be opened to women, including combat units. Last summer Kristen Griest became the first female infantry officer and there will be more like her by late 2016 (*The Washington Post* staff, 2016).

There is truth to the statement that women make less than men over a lifetime because women are more likely to work part-time. Women have long been willing to work fewer hours or for less money for multiple reasons. Some work primarily to procure healthcare benefits since, in the US, healthcare benefits are tied to jobs. Some work fewer hours to accommodate family demands. Part-time can seem like the best way to accommodate both job and family. I've done it myself and it can look like the best of both worlds. However, women are often so grateful to get the arrangement that they do not insist on the compensation that they deserve.

In addition, they may find it much harder to move on to full-time work when full-time income is needed. It is the trend now for employers to avoid giving employees full-time hours in order to avoid giving them benefits. How many people do you know who are scrupulously kept to less than thirty hours per week, or whatever the cutoff is for full-time hours, to avoid giving them sick time or vacation? Keeping employees at part-time allows employers to avoid offering them health insurance, which, under the Affordable Care Act, they must offer to anyone working thirty or more hours (IRS, 2014). It has been said that some employers have systematically cut the hours of their employees for this reason. Or, if they do offer insurance, it is at a much higher rate for part-time workers than for full-time employees. Often, a person has to work two or more part-time jobs in order to survive. If it is hard to balance one job and a family, what is it like with two?

Patrick Gillespie of CNN writes in the *Money* column, "Part-Time Jobs put millions in poverty or close to it," and that "seven million Americans are stuck in part-time jobs." He goes on to say that, since the recession, the rate of people working part-time when they would choose to be working full-time is half again what it was before the crash and that part-time workers are five times more likely that full-time workers to live in poverty. (Gillespie, 2014)

In 2012, according to the Carsey Institute at the University of New Hampshire, one half of the women who involuntarily worked part-time lived below 200% of the poverty line. That would be $23,540 in 2015. The jobs they held did not pay enough for them to live and did not offer real benefits (Frederickson, 2015). Notice the word *involuntarily*. They would like to have full-time work. Full-time has not been offered to them.

Another way employers keep the pay of women low (though not just women) is the newer practice of asking prospective employees to sign waivers stipulating that, if hired, they will never sue their employer for unfair treatment. If they don't sign, they aren't hired. This new subterfuge is in response to class action suits against such as the one vilifying Wal-Mart who had a judgment against them for $188 million in 2014. Employees claimed that they were locked inside the stores after closing in order to stock shelves, a job that sometimes took two hours, though they had already clocked out and were not paid for the extra time. Wal-Mart was also accused of forcing workers to work through mandated breaks and lunches (Reuters, 2014).

I have seen myself the effect of a further weasel word for avoiding overtime. It is called "salaried." Under a law passed by George W. Bush eight million people lost the right to overtime after forty hours of work. That is because employers were allowed, under the new law, to refer to anyone who made $455 per week and had some kind of vague managerial duties to be listed as salaried and, thus, exempt from overtime. President Obama, in 2015, raised the wage level to $970 per week, restoring OT to millions, the majority of them women (CBS, 2015). Of course, real mangers have usually been salaried, but how many real managers do you know who make $455 per week? That is $11.37 per hour for a 40-hour week.

Weasel term two is "Independent Contractor." According to the Bureau of Labor Statistics, this is the fastest growing part of the job market. Though it provides flexibility to the worker, it also provides no traditional coverage such as overtime, health insurance, pay stability or health coverage. My first husband worked as an independent contractor in the construction business. I was able to carry the health insurance through my job and had the stability of full-time. He had several companies who employed him so it worked out, at least in the good times. But what about the hairdresser, the piece worker or the home care workers? As you might surmise, most of these workers are women, and they might have work today — but what about tomorrow?

What if they don't have a working spouse to provide the benefits? How will they get health insurance? They can't even name a figure in advance that they can be sure they will make for the year. *The New York Times* did a piece on "the gig economy." Noam Scheiber contends, "It poses a challenge to the long-standing notion of what it means to hold a job" (Scheiber, 2015).

You may wonder why any women would take a job with no benefits and one so obviously not to her advantage. We do not like to think of class in this country, but a low-paying job is apt to trap a woman into a lower social order. Sociologist Max Weber thinks our measure of equality and inequality is based on four concepts; consumption, prestige, honor and education (Johnson, 2002). I can see why a woman with little education who has never been able to "consume" the more expensive things in life and who has perhaps done nothing but housework, which has long been devalued, would derive some pleasure in a job which labels her a "manager" or an "independent contractor" even if it costs her in the long run.

We do derive a sense of class, an idea of our place in the social order, from our parents and surroundings while we are growing up. Though my mother believed in equality, she also suffered from a sense if inferiority derived from wearing flour sack dresses and being the tenth of eleven children on an Indiana farm. She sometimes declined invitations because she felt that our house wasn't "as good" as the home she might be visiting. She spent most of her life working for someone else before she gained the confidence to take the broker's exam for her real estate license and to become a broker, about forty years past the flour sack dresses.

Our country is one in which children of lower class parents can better themselves financially but the outward appearance of class is harder to learn. Working class parents tend to have working class children and the children of working class parents have a tougher time moving up in the job market than the children of more affluent parents. Manners of dress, speech and knowledge of the outside world or lack thereof can work against a child of working class parents even when he or she has an education equal to others.

One way to judge the difference in the way lower paid women feel about their jobs is the value they place on their contribution. One study found that among women without a high school diploma, the biggest satisfaction they drew from their jobs was "helping to pay the family's bills," and "having my own money," followed by "not having to ask my husband for money." Women with a high school diploma also valued having their own money, but they named a "sense of achievement" as a prime reason for working. This was not often mentioned by women in lower paying jobs (Johnson, 2002). We can probably deduce that paying the bills was the biggest achievement they could expect.

Both middle and working class women have been known to work on an off-and-on basis. This is not wise, as it tends to spoil their chance of advancement if there is one, and it deducts from their payments into Social Security. From personal experience, however, I understand what could motivate these women to give up work for periods of time. Lack of support at home will sap the ambition of any woman, no matter her class.

My then husband refused to do anything to help in the house. I worked in clinics when my children were young to avoid the incompatible hospital hours, weekends and holidays. However, my choice came at a price. My wages were lower and I often had to stay until the doctors were finished for the day. That could be 6 PM. Though it would have been an enormous blessing had my husband cooked, dinner was never started until my son got old enough to do it. My weekends were taken up with laundry, caring for a four-bedroom house and with doing the books for my husband's business. Yes, I did ask for help. We even went to counseling, but he had been raised to equate his manhood with doing only "men's work." He did provide financially for his family, but he felt domestic chores were beneath him. He also did not like for me to work, though it was through my job that we obtained health insurance. When construction was down, my job was the safety net. He objected, as well, when I started taking college courses. There is a hierarchy in the laboratory; first technician with perhaps two years of school, then technologist and supervisor, which required a four-year science degree at that time. I wanted to move up and I did, in time, but it was a much longer slog than it should have been: seventeen years to get a four-year degree. There were times when it was just too much, and I would leave the work force for a matter of months or do some other job to ease the burden. No matter how much you love your work, a bad situation at home can force choices. I feel acutely for any woman in this position and I do know some. Fortunately, the younger generation of men seems to find it more acceptable to help around the house, to cook and do laundry and help with children. I like to think it is because they were raised by working mothers like me and watching television shows that don't stress the old stereotypes.

All the issues previously mentioned effect the pay disparity of women but the most often cited reason is time off for childbirth and childcare. We might have thought we were at least protected from discrimination during pregnancy due to the Pregnancy Discrimination Act of 1978 but even pregnancy gets no slack from some major employers. UPS refused to give light duty to a pregnant employee and the case went all the way to the Supreme Court where UPS was finally forced to allow a pregnant worker light duty when medically indicated (Sneed, 2015). Three of our illustrious Supreme Court Justices still thought the pregnant woman should have to lift and tote as usual, because otherwise she would be treated differently than a man and discrimination regarding women, in their minds, meant that women should be treated, under the law, exactly like men. I liken this to discrimination against a deaf woman. Discrimination regarding her deafness is a separate issue from discrimination regarding her femaleness. Pregnancy is also a condition separate from being female.

Then the pregnant woman gives birth. What support does our society offer her in this crucial time of bonding between mother and child? Currently, the only protection US workers have for keeping their jobs is the Federal Family and Medical Leave Act, FMLA, finally enacted in 1993, which guarantees the worker that a job will be held for twelve weeks while he or she is caring for a new baby or an ill family member. However, this leave is unpaid. In addition, small businesses are exempt. Only businesses with 50 or more workers are covered under the law. The law also only applies to workers who have put in at least 1,250 hours in the previous year for their present employer so short term workers do not qualify (US Dept.. of Labor, 1995). Due to these restrictions, a full 40 percent of American workers do not even fall under FMLA. The issue has become political since Hilary Clinton called for paid family leave as a way of helping women to stay in the workforce. Candidate Bernie Sanders has also advocated for paid maternity leave (Kurtzleben, NPR News, 2015).

Federally mandated paid leave sounds very noble. However, it does not exist yet and a woman making $10 an hour is hurt by losing one day's pay. She can hardly afford to lose twelve weeks. Only 53% of the workers in America report eligibility for any type of paid leave for themselves and only 11% of employers report providing paid family leave (Council of Economic Advisors, 2014). The idea of paid sick and vacation time is reality to only half of us. Human Rights Watch, who we usually think of as reporting on gross miscarriages of justice in foreign lands, weighed in the lack of paid family leave in the United States in a 90-page report, "Failing its Families: Lack of Paid Leave and Work-Family Supports in the US." Parents interviewed for the report said that lack of paid leave contributed to delayed health care for children, postpartum depression for the mothers and abbreviated breast-feeding. Human Rights Watch also contends, "The US is missing out by failing to ensure that all workers have access to paid family leave. Countries that have these programs show productivity gains, reduced turnover costs and health care savings" (Human Rights Watch staff, 2011).

NPR news reporter Danielle Kurtzleben, in her program "It's all Politics," writes about the issue. The US is dead last out of 37 countries outlined in the broadcast for providing paid parental leave. President Obama mentioned in his last State of the Union address that the US is the "only advanced economy that doesn't mandate paid sick or maternity leave for its workers."

The Center for Economic and Policy Research in 2008 addressed the effect of paid and unpaid parental leave on Gender Inequality. "Parental Leave: Gender Equality In the absence of paid parental leave policies, traditional gender roles that involve women as "caregivers" and men as "providers," and the typically lower earnings of mothers (relative to fathers) in the labor market, create strong incentives for women to reduce their employment and take on a large majority of childcare responsibilities. The most obvious problems associated with such outcomes are that women bear a disproportionate burden of childcare responsibilities and pay both a short- and a long-term penalty in the labor market. A related issue is that traditional gender roles and labor-market outcomes work together to deprive men of the opportunity to participate actively in the care of their children (Ray R, Gornich J, Schmitt J, 2008).

I think we can all agree that it is important for new mothers and fathers to have time to recover from childbirth and to bond with the new child. However, in the US, that time comes at a high cost. Many women dread to tell their employers that they are pregnant because they fear repercussions. Despite anti-pregnancy discrimination laws, low wage women in particular are so dependent on their jobs and consequently, on their employers, that they do not dare to ask for leave or for any concession to the demands of pregnancy or motherhood. Sorry to say, there are employers out there who will take advantage of this fear. Many lower income women know that any time lost to pregnancy will make them less likely to receive promotion or even to be retained in their jobs.

Least talked about, but certainly existing, is the attitude that women can reasonably be paid less initially because they "will have to take time off to be having babies." This rationalization is reinforced when a mother asks for flex time or must stay home due to a child's illness. This disregard for working mothers continues to exist in the US because men run by far the majority of large American businesses, and those men are likely to have stay-at-home wives. They cannot conceive of the challenges facing a working mother, yet 71% of mothers with children under the age of 18 worked or were looking for work in 2015 (Cohn, 2014).

Do you see the dichotomy here? It is shameful for American employers to use this cop-out. It was hard, in the lab, when one tech had to call in because her child was sick; but I was fortunate to be working with mostly women, who were mostly mothers, and we did what we needed to do to cover for that absent mom.

It is widely accepted that it is to the betterment of all society for children to have strong family bonds. We pay dearly in poor school performance and juvenile delinquency when parents must put their jobs and the corporate welfare ahead of their families due to dubious employment practices.

Furthermore, both the mother and the father are increasingly taking on parental roles, but it is the mother who most often loses seniority and work longevity because she and her husband have children. The American Association of University Women published their interpretation of the work life of women after they leave school. They found that, ten years after graduation, 23% of mothers were out of the workforce and 17% worked part-time. They also found that when women return to work after staying home with children, employers offered the women lower wages. Fathers, after a child was born to them, did not suffer this penalty. Indeed, many of them received a wage premium. The AAUW refers to the loss of pay and seniority as the "motherhood penalty" (American Assoc. of University Women, 2016).

The US Navy and Marine Corps know this. They have done more to make a career possible for their member mothers than has the private sector. In July of 2015, the Secretary of the Navy, Ray Mabus, announced that they would now allow eighteen weeks of paid maternity leave. The announcement went on the say that "For families, increased time following the birth of her child has tangible benefits for the physical and psychological health of both mother and child. For the Navy and Marine Corps, there is the likelihood that women will return to and stay in their careers yielding higher readiness and retention for the services" (Office of the Chief of Information, 2015).

Perhaps this explains why so many women of ethnic minorities join the military. Black and Hispanic women are subject to an even wider pay gap than are white non-Hispanic women in the general workforce. Hispanic women suffered the largest gap. They earned only 54% of what a white man earned in the US in 2014. Black women made 63% of what a white man earned (American Assoc. of University Women, 2016). Of course, the white men earned more than minority men, too, but that is another story.

If you want to learn about the struggle for equal pay, read *Grace and Grit* by Lilly Ledbetter with Lanier Scott Isom. Ms. Ledbetter began working at Goodyear Tire in 1979. She had already been through other jobs and the trials of being a working mother. Her husband was dissatisfied with having her at work and she agonized over the lack of time she had to devote to her kids, though they, too, enjoyed the financial rewards of her job. She went to Goodyear because it was the best paying job for a girl in small-town Alabama at the time. She describes appalling sexual harassment in the guise of innuendos, remarks on her female anatomy and outright propositions by supervisors to go to bed with them as a price for getting a good performance review. This treatment applied to other women workers in the plant as well as to Lilly. A female co-worker had complained to Lilly because she had been passed over for a promotion. The supervisor told this co-worker that she was not promoted because she was recently married and probably would have kids. I know that it was common, years ago, for a woman to be asked whether she was pregnant or planning to be pregnant, as I was asked this very question in a job interview in 1963.

The turning point for Lilly came when an anonymous person slipped a note to her listing the salaries of the male supervisors with whom she worked as well as her own. In this way, she discovered that she was being paid far less than they were. The highest paid male supervisor was making $59,028 and the lowest was paid $58,226. Lilly was making just $44,724 after being with Goodyear for nearly twenty years.

She filed suit with the Equal Employment Opportunity Commission, EEOC, in 1998 regarding the discrimination and was subsequently threatened with the loss of her job. The woman who had been passed over for promotion, as well as others, turned against her. They all feared the loss of their jobs. Lilly Ledbetter describes how difficult it was to have patience with her family at home when she was under such stress at work. I believe all working mothers can identify with that kind of tension. Lilly took early retirement while she devoted her time to getting ready for the trial. Goodyear tried to smear her by saying her work was not as good as that of the other (male) supervisors, though Goodyear management had given her the Top Performance Award. After an exhausting and prolonged trial, she was awarded over $3,000,000 (Lilly Ledbetter with Lanier Scott Isom, 2012).

Though I am sure this was vindication for Lilly, Goodyear appealed and she never saw the money. Her case was tried before the Supreme Court of the United States and the five-justice majority said that she should have complained sooner if she was being underpaid. Of course, she had no way of knowing that this was the case until she was tipped off. It was a victory for corporate America. Dissenting Justice Ruth Ginsberg said the majority's opinion "didn't make sense in the real world."

Lilly eventually got some movement toward justice when President Obama signed the Lilly Ledbetter Fair Pay Restoration Act, though it has never been ratified by Congress. The Act has been brought before Congress numerous times but is always blocked by the Republican majority.

I suspect that there are many situations today like Lilly's, in which women are blissfully unaware that their male counterparts are being paid more for the same job. *New York* magazine's Ann Friedman advises employers who want to attract and keep great performing female employees, "Pay us enough that if you were to accidentally email the entire office a spreadsheet containing everyone's salary, you wouldn't be ashamed" (*Washington Post* staff, 2016). Well paid workers stay around. This remark is aimed at millennial women who graduated college within the last ten years.

Studies show that women's pay rates began increasing in the 1970s during Lilly's time, a fact that I attribute to the women's movement. We began to aspire to—and to work toward—that "equal pay for equal work" that had so long eluded us. However, that narrowing of the gap began to slow in the 1990s (Blau, Francine and Kahn, Lawrence M, 2007). If the figures used were averages of the total amount earned by women vs. the total amount earned by men, I think I know one reason for the drop. More mothers are not working for some period of time during their careers, and I also think I know why. As will be shown in the following chapters, childcare in the US is very expensive, particularly good childcare, and the dual job of juggling job and family is daunting. A study published by the Bureau of Labor Statistics in 1991 showed that over 40% of young working mothers at that time depended on relatives for childcare, often their own mothers (Gleason, Philip M. and Veum, Jonathan R., 1991). That was

25 years ago. I do not believe that 40% of the working mothers today could be depending on their mothers because their mothers are working, too. In a *New York Times*/CBS News/Kaiser Family Foundation study poll of younger non-working adults, fully 61% of the women said they were not looking for work due to "family responsibilities." Many of these women trained for years for their chosen professions but are not working because of a dearth of support systems. This explains why, in 1990, the United States had one of the highest rates of employment for women but has now fallen behind several European countries (*New York Times* staff, 2015). Mom is not around to take the baby, anymore.

For instance Delphine Dubost, a public school teacher in France, was permitted to return to work at 80% of full-time without a cut in salary. She was also able to enroll her two children in France's state-run daycare system for $740 month including diapers and meals (*New York Times* staff, 2015). Here, in our daycare center for employees in a non-profit healthcare system, the cost would be over $1500 per month (Baycare, 2015).

It seems to me that young women of today do not remember the slogans of feminism or understand the reasons for them. My own daughter, when in the company of my "coming of age in the 70s" friends made the statement that she could not understand why we talked about limitations for women. As far as she could see, women could do anything they wanted now. All five of us "seniors" proceeded to inform her that woman today have those rights because we fought for them. We can never sit back and assume that we will be treated fairly. In today's corporate welfare system, we must be ever more vigilant and ever more vocal.

Women are affected by the gender pay gap in two more ways. The gap affects the finances of women in paying off their student loans. All students pay the same for their education but women take longer to pay back the loans because they make less money and are often obliged to take time off for childbirth and maternity leave. The average student debt for American men in 2007-2008 was $22,656. For women it was $24,126. Four years later, in 2012, the debt still owed was $12,793 for men and $16,105 for women. Only 33% of their debt had been paid off by the women vs. 44% paid off by the men (American Assoc. of University Women, 2016). So now we have the new mother, not only dithering over whether she will be ahead if she returns to work but also about how she is going to retire her student debt if she doesn't. Women took 47% of all law degrees in 2011 and 47% of all medical degrees in 2014 (Baxter, 2015). We can assume that most of them have student debt. Would it not be wise to make it easier for these well-educated professionals to go back to work, knowing their child or children will be well cared for, while the mothers provide the services to society for which they were trained? It would also benefit the taxpayer if they could pay off their student loans.

The other way a lack of wage equity affects women (though not just women) is in lack of retirement savings. Only 40% of Americans in the lower half of the income scale have any form of retirement savings, and even among those who do, their average retirement account totals $40,000. Some who do have access to matching funds for a 401K do not take advantage because they can't afford to have any of their wages withheld, so there is no contribution to be matched. George Lowenstein, a behavioral economist from Carnegie Mellon University with Cazilia Loibl and others did a study to determine why this was the case. He found that they did not save because they simply did not have enough money in their checks to spare the funds (Porter, 2016). If you are just trying to pay the rent, groceries, healthcare, gas and the other expenses of life, retirement seems a long way off and since it feels like a pipe dream, why try to fund it?

In this way, the gender biased pay gap does not stop affecting our lives when we stop working. The *Washington Post* ran an article entitled "Women Fall Short with Nest Eggs" (*The Washington Post*, 2015). The article points out that women in general are better at saving than men are. They are more likely to put money into retirement plans, 73% of women vs. only 66% of men contribute. They also put away a slightly higher percentage of their pay, 7% vs. the 6.8% for men. They are just as likely to invest in stocks and to manage their money well. Yet even the women who can afford to save fall "woefully short" when we look at the retirement fund balances, which are, on average, $79,572 for women and $123,262 for men. The reason given is that, once again, women do not make as much as men. Once again, they may have a shorter tenure, which, we can probably guess, is due to time out for family.

Lastly, women do not insist on equitable pay when it comes to applying for jobs or at promotion. We may not know what the pay should be because we haven't done the necessary research, or we are so grateful to be considered for the position that we don't want to quibble. It seems, sometimes, as though it is only the women of my generation who are still fighting, who remain convinced that change needs to come. Sally Field, only two years my junior, replied recently when asked if women have really come a long way, "We Haven't." "Even in this country, there's not equal pay for equal work. How can anyone justify that? It continues to be brushed under the carpet" (Rhodes, 2016). I know it is enough to make you mad—and we seldom demonstrate our best logic when we are angry.

In her book *The Smart Woman's Guide to Interviewing and Salary Negotiation,* Julie King points out that cursing and raging against an unfair system may serve as venting but does not change the situation, and it can make us look like overwrought harridans. Instead, she suggests taking a critical view of the obstacles in our paths and taking each one in turn. She maintains that men tend to hire people like them, other men. They tend to believe that women can't make tough decisions. The fact is that women make decisions with more thought and less aggression (King J. A., 1995). Witness the hasty and "aggressive" actions by male politicians after the World Trade Center attack and the enormous cost in money and young lives of never ending and not well considered wars. When will we become civilized enough to acknowledge that bald aggression belongs on the sports field, not among human relations?

While Americans in general certainly maintain a higher standard of living that many in the world, it is generally accepted that the wealthy are getting wealthier in the US and the middle class is losing. This is no time to be a shrinking violet. Women have not been raised to insist on asking for what they are worth. If they do, they are labeled as "pushy." The way I see it, if you aren't going to get the raise if you don't ask and you aren't going to get it if you seem pushy, you might as well be pushy. At least you will know you tried rather than go home kicking yourself because you wimped out and trusted your "betters" to give you what you deserve.

Supervisors love for you to leave it in their hands. Jena Mc-Gregor of the *Tampa Bay Times*, Oct. 12, 2014, tells about the CEO of Microsoft, Satya Nadella, who — at an event celebrating women in computing — advised women to "have faith that the system will actually give you the right raises as you go along." He thinks it is "good karma" to trust and not ask for a raise (Mc-Gregor, 2014). Of course, there was a backlash to that statement as many women in the audience had experienced the real world. Even if you have an immediate supervisor who would treat you fairly, they are under the constraint of upper management and the ever-looming bottom line. Some middle managers get bonuses based on how much money they can save the company. The working woman, especially if she is paying childcare, and perhaps not getting the full-time hours she needs, cannot be as concerned with karma as she is with paying the rent.

Finally, there is the satisfaction of working. I stayed at home for a few years after my daughter was born. I was not good at it. I tried but I am not inclined to doing crafts or playing games. I missed the mental stimulation of the laboratory. I have a science bent as many women do and that is not satisfied at home. My whole family was better off if I worked at what I loved. Women should not apologize for wanting to use their talents. What is the alternative, forcing women who have talents in the outside world to remain childless? If we did that, what happens to those genes? Where would the future scientists come from? And how, pray tell, would we staff the hospitals, the restaurants, the offices and retail stores if all the women who are mothers suddenly stayed home?

CHAPTER 5. CHILDCARE SUBSIDIES DISCRIMINATE

Beth Kassab wrote in the *Orlando Sentinel* last year that child-care costs rival the cost of college for many parents. (Kassab, 2015). She gives the average cost for infant care as $173 per week. For a fifty-week year, excluding vacation weeks, that is $8,650 for a child less than one year old, though it can be higher. The yearly cost is $8,300. The average tuition quoted for a state university is $6,300/yr. I'm sure many new parents sit down with pen and calculator and try to figure out if they will come out ahead after paying for infant care if the mother returns to work. They probably feel that, so long as there is a little something left after the childcare is paid, that little something can go toward the rent, the mortgage or the car payment or maybe the health care coverage is coming from her check. Without it, there will be no health care coverage.

Another consideration is job security. We have already established that the employer (even if the FMLA law covers them) need only hold a job for twelve weeks. If the new mother does not return to work after that time, she risks losing her seniority, her pay grade and she will be falling behind in any job involving technical expertise.

And what consideration is given to the working mother at the end of the year when tax time comes around? The income tax provisions for helping parents are confusing. There is Child Tax Credit available to all parents, working and other wise that does not involve daycare cost (IRS, 2014). Since it is available to everyone with a child seventeen or younger, I will not discuss it here. Pertinent to our discussion is the childcare tax credit (IRS, Publication 503, 2014) for any child under the age of thirteen, at which time the government seems to decide that a child does not need watching. We know better, but that's another issue. The childcare tax credit uses a limit of $3000 for one child or $6000 for two as the beginning of the calculation. This in itself is inadequate, as it falls far short of that $8,300 for infant care alone that we just mentioned. Of course, there is further cost for two young children. In 2012, NACCRRA, the National Association of Childcare Resource and Referral, gives a figure of $6,368/yr. for the cost of daycare for a four-year-old child. If a mother has an infant and a three-year-old, she could be paying out as much as $14,668 a year in childcare and it is very possible to pay more (National Association of Childcare Resource and Referral, 2012). The Tax credit for childcare is a percentage based not only on how much you paid for care but also on your income.

Beth, a mother on her own with two qualifying children, has an income of $15,000 per year, about $7 an hour. She can claim up to 35% of the amount she paid for childcare for two children and wind up with no tax burden at all. If the credit is more than she is liable for in taxes, she does not get a refund of the difference. It is limited to the amount of taxes that actually apply to her income.

Barbara is a mother with two kids of the same age. She makes $43,000 per year, about $20 an hour. She can only use a figure of 20% of her earned income in figuring the credit. If her gross income is $43,000, 20% is $8600, but she can only use the $6000 allowed for two children. Using standard deduction her tax burden will probably also be wiped out, a saving of two to three thousand dollars. The difference is that she paid out $14,668 to be able to work. With an income of $43,000, Barbara, unlike Beth with her lower income, has paid the whole childcare load herself. A woman with two children with an income above $40,180 is not eligible for subsidized childcare (Florida's Office of Early Learning, 2015), a subject we will now visit. The higher paid mom is still financially ahead of the person making $15,000 per year, but not as far ahead as you might think.

The statistics for 2012, the latest available for NACCRRA, show 14,708,600 children under age six potentially needing childcare in the US. They show 5,572,093 working mothers of children under six. (National Association of Child Care Resources and Referral, 2012) Let us look at what these various mothers are actually paying.

The main agency funding subsidized childcare in Florida is The Early Learning Coalition, ELC, administered as the School Readiness program. It is funded both by the federal and state governments. Parents must be working and/or attending school (college or trade) at least 20 hours a week in order to qualify. Parents must pay a copayment, which is based on a sliding scale. The scale varies according to family income and family size. Funding is primarily to help low-income families but also covers childcare for homeless parents, parents who are victims of domestic violence, teenage parents, families of children with disabilities and others. A family of four can make up to 200% of the federal poverty level, and still qualify for some subsidized childcare. The federal poverty level for 2015 is $11,770 yearly (US Dept. of Health and Human Services, 2015) and 200% of that is $23,540. In a West Florida county, a single mother making that amount would pay only $4 per child per day if that child were enrolled in a day care center that accepts ELC. A single mother of two who is making $40,180 yearly would pay $14 per child per day in the same center. A single mother and two children with an income above $40,180 is not eligible for ELC subsidy and will pay as much as the $34 per day, per child, mentioned earlier. It doesn't give much incentive for a raise in pay, does it, if a mother will lose her childcare subsidy for a few dollars more?

Also, there is no guarantee that there will be space in an ELC program for an eligible child. Certainly, not all childcare providers accept ELC. There is a lot of paperwork and the state does not pay them what they may be able to get from private pay parents (Florida Childcare and Development Fund, 2014–2015). In 2013, a wait list of 75,000 children was reported for subsidized childcare in Florida. That list has since diminished but at any one time, there may be no space in your particular area (Sherman, 2013).

The only time the US government tried to make childcare widely available is during World War II. Because they needed American women to work in the factories making goods for the war effort, the Lanham Act was passed in 1940 to set up government run childcare centers. The centers only served 13% of the children needing care. Nevertheless, the experiment proves that government run childcare is possible and the need for it surely remains. One legislator, referring to the Lanham Act, is quoted as saying, "You cannot have a contented mother working in a war factory if she is worrying about her children and you cannot have children running wild in the streets without a bad effect on the coming generations" (Cohen, 1996). How is this not true today? I so wish that those childcare centers could have stayed open and qualified teachers had been retained to serve the needs of future parents. Instead, there were vocal critics of the idea of childcare outside the home. Frances Perkins, Secretary of Labor, wrote to the head of the Children's Bureau in 1942, asking, "What are you doing to prevent the spread of the day care nursery, which I regard as the most unfortunate reaction to the hysterical propaganda of recruiting women workers?" (Frederickson, 2015) It is fair to say that the nurseries might not have been the best and Sec. Perkins was most concerned with children.

Another effort was made in the 1970s to provide government childcare with the proposal of the Child Development Act of 1971, with appropriate funding for building or buying childcare facilities, with care to be offered on a sliding scale. The original intent was to reach more children, but right wing objectors, associating childcare with the women's rights movement, lobbied to block the program. Phyllis Schafly became a household name, claiming that providing women with childcare would "change our laws, our textbooks, our constitution, our military, everything — and end up taking our husbands' jobs away." (Frederickson, 2015)

Now, almost 45 years later, we are still having to listen to women on television, most of whom have never worked, nor ever needed to, telling all women that we should be completely content to stay at home with our children and we need not expect any help if we choose to do otherwise. It has always been an enigma to me that these same women criticize Welfare mothers who do choose to stay at home with their children. Women can't win!

As I stated in my prologue, I am fully in support of subsidies. I volunteer in a domestic abuse shelter. The women there are expected to find jobs, arrange for a place to live, transportation, childcare, etc. Most of the women are not trained in specific careers and must start with entry-level jobs. Some take jobs waitressing, but tips are not dependable and the hours may not be compatible with raising children.

One job which will sometimes allow for on-the-job training or hospital-paid training is that of a nurse's aide, now called Patient Care Technician. The average pay for a PCT in the US is $12.44 per hour (Payscale, Human Capital, 2015). That's $25,875 for a 52-week year. At this rate of pay, a single mom with young children would definitely qualify for subsidies. At an ELC daycare, our PCT will pay about $25 per week for each child for childcare. They'll get by, but, because she wants more for her kids, she may consider going back to school.

Taking classes while you are working and responsible for young children is not easy, but it has been done. So consider this ambitious young PCT. We'll give her a name, Mary. Mary thinks about becoming an LPN. The average pay for an LPN is $40,288 per year. With an ELC cutoff of $40,180, Mary, as an LPN, would lose her childcare subsidy. One of the largest hospital groups in my area offers on-site daycare. The fee for infant care for a team member is $218 per week, and for a three-year-old, it's $167 per week minus a $5 discount for the second child (Baycare, 2015). We now have the mother who is entitled to subsidized care paying $50/week for care for her infant and her three-year-old in an ELC accepting daycare and Mary, as an LPN, paying $380 for the same age children at her place of work. At that rate, she would be forking out $19,000 per year for childcare. Subtracted from her salary, that would leave $22,288 remaining from her gross pay for the year as an LPN. As a PCT, she paid out $2500 in childcare. Subtracted from her yearly wage as a PCT, she was left with $23,375 for the year, more than she would have as an LPN. Is it worth the effort for Mary to go back to school and shoulder the increased responsibility of an LPN? For personal satisfaction, probably; for future advancement, yes; for financial gain at this stage in her life, it doesn't look like it.

I bring these figures to life not to dissuade any woman from bettering herself, nor to criticize the lower paid worker for taking advantage of subsidies, but rather to point out that the rules are arbitrary. As we will see in future chapters, cutoffs as they exist are unjust. There should not be an abrupt cutoff for subsidized childcare. The scale should continue on into higher paid categories, with the higher paid moms paying more for care, yes; but not so much that it negates their gain.

We have not talked about quality of care. There are licensed daycare centers and there are accredited daycare centers. This is the description per the Early Learning Website (Coalition, 2015).

Licensing Versus Accreditation – What Is the Difference?

Most childcare providers are licensed and some are licensed and accredited. What is the difference?

Licensing is when a facility meets the minimum standards required by Florida's Department of Children and Families (DCF) for a childcare program to be open for business. These requirements include minimal standards for health and safety, ratio, group size and more. *Accreditation* means that the childcare provider has met higher quality standards, usually set by a national organization. These childcare programs have met standards beyond those established by DCF. Accredited programs seek to offer the best quality of care for your child.

For childcare centers, there are many different types of accreditation, for example NAEYC, APPLE, NACECEP, and others. For family childcare homes, accreditation is done through the National Association for Family Childcare (NAFCC).

The NAFCC has a forty-six page list of requirements for being accredited (NAFCC, 2013, fourth edition). The requirements for the others are also daunting. Childcare Centers who accept ELC do not make lots of money. Likely, they can't pay their staff as much and perhaps do not offer as much in the way of teaching as their private pay counterparts. As you might expect, daycare centers that accept ELC will probably not be as highly accredited, though I'm sure there are exceptions.

Often there is not enough time for teaching in an ELC daycare, and it is no wonder. Limiting subsidized care to the lowest paid people creates a mound of paperwork, requiring proof of income, number of people in the household, etc. Not only is it unfair, it is inefficient. In 2013 in Pinellas County, Florida, $2.4 million in federal and state funds was forfeited back to the funders because ELC did not get the people signed up who needed the care within the required time period — and they were many (Phillips, 2013). Extending the limits of eligible income and instituting a system whereby parents could be pre-approved, perhaps via income tax returns, would make it easier on the registrar at the daycare and would probably also avoid some fraud.

You may remember the Child Development Act of 1971, so villainized by Phyllis Schlafly. The bill did not only provide for a national network of childcare centers with tuition depending on family income. The idea was to fund meals, medical checkups and staff training (Badger, 2014). Can you imagine? A working mother would not have to take time off from her job for a well-baby check because it would have been done at the day care center by trained staff. More and more mothers were working at the time, and both Democrats and Republicans supported the bill. However, Pat Buchanan wielded influence in the White House at the time and when the Child Development Act of 1971 came before him, President Nixon, who had originally supported the idea, withdrew his support, saying that the government should not raise children in place of their parents. The idea was even likened, in Buchanan's words, to the "Sovietization of American children" and further misinformation followed, including the fear that daycare facilities could lead to "government indoctrination of small children" (Badger, 2014). We have never come so close again to the kind of assistance American women need in the childcare arena.

Nor has the government helped as much as it should to make after school care available. In 2016, *The Tampa Bay Times* ran an article about the Florida legislature, which refused to give millions more in aid to non-profit groups that wanted to run some of Florida's after school programs. The Legislature opted, instead, to remain with the few groups that have received preferential treatment for decades. Boys and Girls Clubs will remain as a provider, though their funding was cut. Many other groups with after-school programs to offer did not get a chance to bid for taxpayer funds. These funds are supposed to pay for homework help and mentoring (Clark, 2016). Boys and Girls Clubs may very well provide good after school care, but they are not available everywhere. I picked my older grandsons up from after-school care many times and they were usually sitting in an overcrowded lunchroom enveloped in a cacophony of noise. I saw no homework being done, nor did that seem possible amidst the deafening clamor and general confusion.

When are we going to get serious about getting the best care possible for our kids and for getting the younger ones ready for school? If the government is going to be part of this childcare enterprise, let them do it right. Fund quality day care centers and let everyone participate on a real sliding scale that rewards advancement. Everyone would benefit if there were not two separate entities, those who pay through the nose for care they may consider better and those who take what they can get because they can't afford anything else.

Chapter 6. Work or Welfare, Who Fares Best?

I have learned much about how things work in the world of government subsidies since I began volunteering in a Domestic Abuse facility. Since Shelter rules require that women look for housing and employment while in the safe house, we do provide access to a computer and we take them to a local employment service that lists jobs available and tries to match people with work. If the women are obliged to take entry-level work and they have young children, we also make them aware of the Early Learning Coalition and determine what subsidies are possible and whether there are openings at participating daycare centers. Next, the advocates tackle transportation. Most of the women do not have cars. Bus schedules do not always accommodate job hours and the same bus often does not carry the mom to both the daycare center and her job. Many of the women start out optimistic. We have a storage facility where we keep donations of clothes and household items. Time after time, I have watched a client hunt through the racks and find clothes acceptable for an interview, meet the employer's representative, get the job — and then reality steps in. She finds out how much she will have to pay for childcare and whether there is a waiting list. She deals with finding a place to live beyond her six weeks at the shelter, what she will be paying in rent, how she can get from her home to work and daycare, and whether she will qualify for food stamps. The math is sobering, and then another client says, "Why even work? I get along better than that on public assistance."

Let's begin with food stamps. To be eligible for food stamps, a woman with two children could make up to $40,180/yr. before taxes in 2015 and still be eligible for an EBT, Electronic Benefit Transfer card (formerly issued as food stamps) from the program known as SNAP (Florida Dept. of Children and Families, 2015). That salary breaks down to $19.31/hr. Most of the clients at our shelter cannot hope to make that much here in Florida. For example, let's go back to Mary, the Patient Care Tech with the two children that we talked about before. At $12.44/hr., $25,875/yr., she will certainly qualify for food stamps. With three in the family, she could get about $511 per month in assistance with nutrition (USDA, 2015) — probably not enough to pay for food for three people for a month but a big help. Now she looks at rent. At the shelter, we have applications for subsidized housing. HUD housing uses a formula based on gross annual income minus some deductions (Dept.. of Housing and Urban Development, 2015). Mary would get a deduction of $480 for each of her three dependents. That amounts to $1440 deducted from her annual salary of $25,875. Her HUD rent is calculated as 28–30% of her gross monthly income after the deductions. Deducting the allowed $1440 from her salary and dividing by 12, her adjusted monthly income is $2,036.25. Thirty percent of $2,547.25 is $610.87. She could pay about $611/month for rent so long as she qualifies for subsidized housing.

There is a new MAGI formula that supposedly makes the calculation of rent simpler. In order to be accurate, I called the Housing and Urban Development answer line, which is posted on their website. The woman who answered could not answer my question but gave me the number of the local Housing Authority. I called the Housing Authority and left a message but received no call back. The next day, I again called the answer line, was again told that they could not answer my question, was again given the number of the Housing Authority in New Port Richey, FL. I called them again, left another message and again received no call back. I am truly sorry for anyone who needs government help with housing.

Since I could not get further information, for purposes of comparison we will use the old calculation for our two mothers. Mary is paying $10/day for subsidized daycare for the two children, $220 plus per month. Almost half of her roughly 2000/month pay is going for rent and daycare and she still has to pay for transportation, medical insurance, utilities and what food the EBT card does not cover. The average cost for water and sewer in our part of Florida varies between $96 and $107 (Pasco County Utilities, 2014; Pinellas County Utilities, 2016). We can use $100 as an average. The average monthly electricity usage in Florida is 911 KWH/month (US Energy Administration, 2015). This is probably low due to the need for air conditioning so we will use 1000 KWH. The rates charged locally in Florida are complicated, consisting, as they do, of basic charges, per KWH charges and fuel surcharges but 1000 KWH should run our single mother about $111 per month (Duke Energy, 2015). She has now spent all but $962 of her monthly pay and we have not taken out any taxes. Mary may not have much, if any, income tax withheld as she has three dependents and qualifies as Head of Household. She also qualifies for the Earned Income Credit but she will still have deductions for Social Security and Medicare deducted from her pay. That amounts to about $155 per month (IRS, Topic 751, 2015). So, deduct $155 from her monthly $962. That leaves $807. Now, let us look at health insurance. The income limit, at the time, to qualify for Medicaid, using a family of three, is $2,309 (Center for Medicare and Medicaid Services, 2014). At her monthly income of $2036, she has squeaked by. However, once again, she will not be getting ahead if she eventually makes an extra $275/month because she will lose her Medicaid.

How is she going to get to work and to the daycare? If she could take a bus from our shelter, the best deal is an unlimited ride adult pass for $37.50 for 31 days and two $18.75 children's passes for 31 days (Pasco County, 2015). That's $75/month. If the bus goes where she needs to go and at a time when she needs to be there, that is cheaper than having a car.

Of course, it is more convenient to have one's own car. It is doubtful that Mary would have either the cash for a car or for the sales tax and tag, so all of that would have to be financed if she were to become a car owner. She would have to have the credit to get the loan. She would then have to find insurance. Several new residents of Florida have told me that Florida's rates are higher than those of some other states. Mary would likely have to pay the insurance over time, resulting in finance cost; and we haven't touched on maintenance. This will not be a new car. Research by AAA in 2015 gives a figure of $8698 per year for the total cost of owning and operating a small sedan including insurance (Stepp, 2015). That seemed high until I remembered what the cost was, per month, when I had a car payment and was working every day. The AAA figure assumes that the car owner will be driving 15,000 miles per year. If Mary's job is only ten miles from her home and the daycare is only five miles out of the way, she will travel only about 10,000 miles a year. AAA breaks down their estimate to 58 cents for each mile driven so Mary will spend about $483/mo. for car expense if she gets her own car and sticks to the 10,000 miles.

So now, we subtract the transportation cost from her remaining $807 and Mary is down to $324/month after rent, childcare and transportation. Mary will likely not get by on the $511/month that she gets in Food Assistance. In 2013, *USA Today* printed an article allowing that it costs $191 per week for a family of four for a low-cost food plan (Hellmich, 2013). That is almost $50 per person per week and that was three years ago. Mary will almost certainly have to kick in for food and an EBT card does not cover toiletries, pet foods or paper products. So Mary has $324/month, just over $10 per day divided between three people, for clothes, over the counter health products, grooming and personal necessities, paper towels, toilet paper, tissues, the occasional Happy Meal, birthdays, Christmas and any entertainment.

Now let's consider Susan, who was in the Shelter with Mary and pointed out to her that she might consider Public Assistance. Susan also has two young children, an infant and a three-year-old. She is entitled to TANF (Temporary Assistance to Needy Families) because she has a child under the age of 18 and an income less than 185% of the federal poverty level (previously listed as $11,770/year for 2015 (Florida Dept.. of Children and Families, 2012). Her maximum cash benefit for a family of three in Florida is listed as $303/month (*Singlemother's Guide*, 2015). She is entitled to the same food EBT benefits as Mary, $511/month. Susan's TANF qualifies as her income. She qualifies for public housing under HUD with a rent of about $50/month and she can deduct from her reported income any money she pays for child-care while looking for a job or doing community service (Dept. of Housing and Urban Development, 2015). She will be staying home with her own children so there is no childcare expense. There is a requirement, under TANF, that participants put in a certain number of hours working, preparing for a job, in community service or watching the children of someone who is participating in these endeavors. In order to fulfill this requirement, she may have a relative or friend who can watch her children. If she doesn't, she can leave her children in subsidized childcare while looking for work, etc., at the minimum rate of as little as $1 day.

Susan will definitely get Medicaid. She does not need regular transportation. She can ride the bus for $1.50 one way. She pays no taxes. Susan can apply for LIHEAP, Low Income Home Energy Assistance Program that helps with utility costs (Children and Families Administration, 2016). For groceries not covered by EBT, she is eligible, by virtue of being on public assistance, to get items at the food pantries. Adopt a Family recommendations come from those same food pantries, meaning it is Susan's family who is eligible to be adopted by a church or work group who will provide them with a Christmas list fulfilled, free of charge. When the rent of $50 is subtracted from Susan's $303, Susan has about $250 remaining. If we allow her $100 a month for extra food, bus fare and incidentals, she has only about $150 left, not much for sure, but Mary had only a little more than $300 remaining and she was obliged to leave her children in order to work. She got up early every morning, negotiated day care, gave bed baths, carried bed pans and dealt with all the household chores in the evening — chores that Susan has all day to do.

I don't want to make it to sound like Susan is living in luxury. Welfare moms do not fare well. They live on a pittance and they are allowed to get TANF for only two years at a stretch, four to five years in a lifetime. She and Mary are both subject to the disdain of some people in the grocery line when they pull out their

EBT cards. I have seen people actually peruse the groceries on the belt to see if there isn't some item there that this subsidized family could do without. At least, Mary has the self-esteem of working and some measure of self-determination. Susan doesn't have a car. She probably gets bored staying home with little kids all day.

I have noticed how few of the mothers in our shelter spend much one-on-one time with their children. It is likely that, in their own childhoods, they were not given this attention themselves. Poverty begets poverty. An article in *The Tampa Bay Times* quotes Lindsay Carson, CEO of the Early Learning Coalition of Pinellas County, FL, "Children in poverty tend to receive lower quality childcare, stunting their intellectual growth. By the time they enter school, they are already behind. From there the disparities keep building. The risks of drug and alcohol addiction, teen pregnancy and run-ins with law enforcement rise (Johnston, 2015). Susan is not in a good place.

Of course, some women make better salaries. I will introduce Vickie. Vickie is an RN, single and has two children, an infant and a four year old but Vickie makes $63,000/year (Payscale, Human Capital, 2015). Her monthly income of $5,250 is above the limit for subsidized daycare. Her taxes for the month are about $664 (Intuit, 2016). Her Social Security and Medicare tax amount to another $286 (US Social Security Administration, 2015), so her take home for the month is $4,300. Her childcare costs are about $1,600 per month using the in house childcare provided by her employer (Baycare, 2015). Vicky does not qualify for SNAP (food stamps) as she makes more than the $40,180 limit (Florida Dept. of Children and Families, 2015). She might expect to pay approximately the $50/week per person given above, that is $600/month, for food (Hellmich, 2013). That figure is low if she has to buy formula. She also makes too much for housing assistance so her rent will be at least $1000 / month and that is only for a two-bedroom unit (Realtor.com, 2016). We can assume that she will pay at least the same for utilities and car as our other mothers paid, so there goes another $694. At the end of the month, Vickie is left with $406, working full-time as an RN with all the attendant educational requirements, responsibility and stress. That isn't a lot more than Mary winds up with and Mary is killing herself for $150 per month more than Susan gets.

Vickie looked ahead and got an education, which allows her to live without assistance. However, she is paying dearly for that option in both the expense she will bear alone and in the challenges of her job. Both Mary and Susan are poor and they both have faced tough choices. Mary chose to work and is obliged to leave her young children in a daycare center that is possibly not the best quality. Do you wonder, at this point, why Susan chose welfare? Self-sufficiency is wonderful but when a new mother is faced with having to leave that tiny infant and her young child in a daycare, the idea of being able to stay home with them for two years on public assistance must look pretty darn good. Again, it shouldn't be either/or. We should have paid maternity leave. We should make subsidized childcare available to everyone, even Vickie, with cost depending on income.

By virtue of her low wages, Mary would also qualify for some of the food pantries and church sponsored giveaways I mentioned but they are seldom open during the hours when Mary could apply and could stand in line to collect. She may not even know that they exist. She's too busy getting the kids to school or daycare, getting the laundry done, groceries bought, food prepared and the myriad other chores that a single parent faces. Vickie also deals with the same challenges every day and she would not qualify for most charity programs.

Certainly, moms like Vickie and Mary who choose to "do it all" deserve more recognition. The abrupt cutoff for childcare fees is punishing for working mothers. Food pantries should make sure struggling working moms get some of the free food and some of those gifts at Christmas. At my Quaker Meeting, we have decided to choose our next adoptive family from the rolls of the subsidized daycare and give a free Christmas to a mom who works every day.

At this point, I'm sure that there will be some who say, "Well, why are these women having children when they don't have an adequate way to support them?" There are both simple and complicated answers to that question. Most women want children. It is a basic biological urge. It is also true that most of the women who wind up in these circumstances come from families who also had children early and unplanned. It is not a matter of reason to them. It is just something that happens and I have never met one expectant mother, even though she was living in a shelter and had suffered abuse, who didn't look forward to having her baby. Mitt Romney was quoted as saying, at a commencement address, that for those who graduate from high school, get a full time job and marry before they have their first child, the probability that they will be poor is 2%. If all of these conditions are absent, the probability is 76% (Yglesias, 2012). I have no doubt that this statistic is true but the author of this same article goes on to say that teen mothers do not remain poor because they had a baby. Instead, Mr. Yglesias believes that they have a baby because they are poor. I think he is on to something.

A baby is something new and exciting. While pregnant and at the time of childbirth, the mother is given a lot of attention. She usually has the baby in the same hospital as mothers who are not teens, not single and not poor. If the father is the type of man who equates manhood with how many babies he can father, she will get attention from him. We are talking girls who have not had much attention here. If their mothers worked, the moms probably had jobs that did not give much in the way of satisfaction or validation. If they were on welfare themselves, no doubt the babies they brought into the world provided the only bright spots in their existence, too. Poor school performance is unfortunately the norm among poor children, not because they are born less intelligent (though there may be instances where this is the case such as having lead in the drinking water). Rather, it is because they all too often have not received the intellectual stimulation necessary to thrive in school. Reading is crucial for classroom success and it is not a natural function. ASCD, a teaching organization says that reading skill requires attention, focus and motivation in the home. In their study, only 36% of low-income parents read to their child while 62% of upper income parents did (Jensen, 2009). This is partly because a parent has no time left after working long hours to provide a basic living and partly because that parent was not read to herself and does not see the need to read to her child. Children from lower socio-economic homes receive less access to other kinds of learning opportunities, less access to computers, fewer books and more time watching TV not of educational value. This kind of deprivation is known to lead to disassociation with school and disassociation is known to lead to teen pregnancy (Manlove, 2010). Girls who have failed one or two grades in school do not set their sights high. Teen girls interviewed for the book *Getting by on the Minimum* said they were tired of failing, bored and ready to get on with "real life" (Johnson, 2002). These young girls do not see the value in school. They have not grown up in a home where education has been achieved and rewarded. Many have seen or themselves been the victims of abuse. They search for a way to get away from home, to start over. What they have seen is the reward, albeit transient, that other young mothers get from their babies. Babies appear doable to these girls. A college education and rewarding career do not.

We must not forget that many fine and productive men and women come from homes with teen mothers, single mothers and welfare mothers. Certainly, it would be better if they were educated before becoming mothers and before choosing men who do not make good fathers. I am sure they know that, too, after the fact. However, the children are already here. We can't send them back. We can do a better job of making education meaningful to working class kids, of offering job training in high school, of making contraceptives available early on, of teaching life skills. Every ninth grader should be learning how much rent will cost, childcare and groceries, how much jobs really pay and then let them do the math.

We haven't touched on fathers. I have heard the question asked many times and I have asked it myself, "Why don't these women expect more from the fathers of their children?" Why are they content to let him go his separate way, in many cases fathering more children, while they are left with the kids and no help from him? After my several years at the shelter, I've answered my question. The mothers don't ask for more because they don't think they are worth more. These women feel that they can't get anything else. They feel that they have failed at school, at preparation in general. They accept whatever love and validation they are given, even when it is false. They have lost hope — or they never had any.

Many of our clients at the shelter are not married or are not married to the father of their child. It is more complicated to qualify for public assistance if a woman is married or living with the father of her child. The number of work hours required will be increased in a two-parent family. If he does not work the hours required, she can lose her TANF benefit (Florida Dept.. of Children and Families, 2016). If she names the father but is not married to him, the state will expect him to pay child support. As I said earlier, Florida goes after deadbeat dads when they reach a certain dollar level of back support. If they don't pay up, they might lose their driver's license or even wind up in jail. However, that only works if the dad has a job and a bank account that can be monitored. If the TANF applicant's husband or boyfriend decides to skip out, work in another state under a different Social Security number, work "under the table," or simply not work at all, she will have to apply again as a single applicant. Of course, he should be carrying half the load; but if he can't be made to do so, it seems reasonable to prepare the mother to carry it. Making it possible for her to work and removing the arbitrary subsidy limits that discourage her from moving up would be a great start.

CHAPTER 7. BEST FIT IN JOBS FOR WOMEN AND FOR MOTHERS

Forbes magazine lists twenty of what they consider to be the best-paying jobs for women. Listed are Orthodontist, Physicist, Attorney, Economist and, in the Health professions: Nurse Practitioner, Pharmacist, Nurse Anesthetist. Physicians of different types were listed. There are various kinds of engineer such as Petroleum, Sales, Electrical and Architectural. These jobs command salaries of from $87,000 to $137,000 per year and more (Dill, 2015). I don't doubt that these are good professions or that women are fully capable of doing them. However, every one requires long years of school, probably post graduate, and most require a proclivity for science and math. Perhaps you aren't willing to go to school for that long or to rack up that much student debt. So, what can you do with a bachelor's degree?

The most oft-mentioned jobs for graduates with bachelor's degrees are in the computer industries, particularly web developers and software developers. These jobs would probably have compatible hours and pay well, $65,000 to $100,000 annually (US News staff, 2016). Web design is in high demand as the Internet is the first place many of us look when we need information on a business, government agency or just to see the news. Nearly every business uses computer software, and the software engineer must be familiar with the business if he or she is to design software that actually works. Medical Technologists with whom I have worked have gone into the business of writing laboratory software. Restaurants are increasingly using computer software. Insurance companies rely on their own kind of program. There is really no end to the kinds of software that will be needed in the future. With the right creativity and computer skills, there is also the opportunity to go out on your own. Imagine the designers of video games.

There is no reason why a woman could not do repair on computers and related equipment. In the clinical laboratory, some of the service techs and many of the people responsible for implementing new instruments and software are women. If you want to work on personal computers and smaller devices, you have the option of setting up your own shop. One consideration, if you choose to go into the repair of medical devices, is that it will not be a 9–5:00 job. If an instrument break down in the lab at 2 AM, the technologist on duty will do as much as possible to make a repair. If that doesn't work, the service tech will be dispatched as soon as possible thereafter, probably very early. That would be a consideration in the case of the single mother of small children.

If you like numbers and keeping things orderly, accounting is still a viable career, paying about $65,000 and up. Alternatively, consider statistician. Who do you think computes all the cumulative records of sports teams and players? Statisticians also keep track of sales for businesses, helping them decide what items are selling and where. The Dept.. of Labor expects growth in this area and it is understandable. Environmental statistics need to be compiled for the purpose of wildlife management.

Data must be kept and analyzed in the area of public health and safety. An increase in accidents or illness may initially show up in properly kept public health records. A doctor may notice an increase of a certain kind of cancer in his patient base, and scrutiny of the statistics for past years may lead him or another person to find out that the incidence of cancer correlated with the opening of a dump site or an incinerator. Statisticians make about $80,000 yearly. Similar skills are needed for an Operations Systems or Research Analyst. This job involves figuring out how many people are required for a project, how products can most efficiently be moved to market or where the problem is in a supply line. Operations Analysts also make up to $80,000/yr. and the hours would be reasonable (US News staff, 2016).

Many students graduate with a degree in Business with various specialties. Banks, investment services and insurance companies hire Financial Services Sales Agents. They provide the information on stocks and bonds, annuities and mutual funds. The pay would be about $68,000/year but many of these agents are eligible for commissions on sales.

Marketing is a growing field and can pay well if you have an outgoing personality and enthusiasm. Though the pay is not that great to start, perhaps $40,000, if you really get familiar with your product and follow up on every question and sale, you can work your way into a very lucrative career that does not have you out in the middle of the night.

Managers of all types work in retail stores, auto sales, property management and corporate offices. A degree in Business is also a good way to prepare if you want to start your own company. In their book, Joan Williams and Rachel Dempsey give advice to women entering business and in particular, management. They recommend finding a special niche that you do particularly well. Learn all there is to know about one product line or one process. You will soon find yourself the go-to person for that product or process and will become as near to being indispensable as it is possible to get. Remember, also, their stereotypical definition of what is needed in a manager: leadership, assertiveness, sound judgment and the ability to take control and make tough decisions . This may sound daunting, but I really believe that some, if not all, of these qualities can be learned; and self-confidence is the first lesson you need to master.

Human Resource management jobs usually pay about $55,000 annually. The HR person is often the first representative of a company and you need to develop a welcoming attitude. Likewise, if you like dealing with people, there are jobs such as school psychologists and substance abuse counselors. The pay is about $65,000 yearly and would no doubt offer a lot of personal satisfaction if you could help young people to find the right path in life or if you could be instrumental in defeating an addiction (Create a Career staff, 2013).

Don't forget about government jobs. There are many and the benefits are good. My friend worked for many years for OSHA, the Occupational and Health arm of the US government, and there is now a degree in that specialty. Local governments hire health and safety engineers, inspectors, computer specialists and many other jobs requiring only a four-year degree or even less.

Projected job growth is perhaps highest in Health Care. With an aging population, there are many behind the scenes positions such as nutritionist, $55,000 yearly or more, or hospital administrator, paying at least $69,000 per year. Both of these jobs require at least a Bachelor's degree and a more advanced degree may be preferred (Create a Career staff, 2013). There are lots of jobs for nurses and for medical technologists but we will consider them when we speak of jobs for the working mother.

Of course, teaching is attainable too, with a four-year degree, but it is not an easy job. Teachers today have to maintain control in a classroom with widely disparate students who do not all value learning. They also have work to do at home in the evening; and educational policy, particularly in Florida, is constantly changing. Many teachers wonder whether it is worth the effort for the possible $54,000 they will make in a year (*US News* staff, 2016). On the plus side, there is June, July and August when time can be devoted to other activities.

Higher education is not for everyone. Many very intelligent people do not like school or find a lot of "book learning" to be unnecessary for what they want to do. If you don't have a Bachelor's degree, there are many jobs available with an Associate's degree or a Certificate. Two positions in health care, with multiple jobs available at present, are Occupational or Physical Therapy Assistant. Being an assistant does not pay as well as being a registered OT or PT, but your training can be completed in four or five semesters and the pay is about $55,000 yearly.

Another booming field is Dental Hygienist. The median salary for a dental hygienist is about $71,000/year. Training to be an LPN (Licensed Practical Nurse) can be completed in one to two years and, though there are still many Baccalaureate degrees in Nursing, many of the registered nurses today are graduating from two-year degree programs. The hospital system where I worked paid them while they were doing their internship.

One small detail has been omitted when we talk about education. That is the cost of getting one. If you want to go to school for any of these jobs, how do you finance it? The cost of one credit hour at one of our local community colleges runs an average of $108. At the closest state university, the cost is $185 per credit hour. A single course consists of at least three credit hours. If you are trying to go to school part-time, taking, perhaps, two courses per semesters, that will be a minimum of $648 in tuition plus the books which often run $100 each. If your parents can afford the tuition and books, perhaps living expenses, too, you are a fortunate woman. Student loans are almost always available but they have to be repaid and, if you are a single woman or even a young married, you will not want that extra expense if you can avoid it.

I've already pointed out that it takes women longer to repay their loans because, in general, they don't make as much money to start with. The most advantageous way to finance your education is with a Pell grant from the US government. They are intended to pay for either college or vocational school. To get a Pell grant, you must be a US citizen or have a green card. You must have a high school diploma, a GED or have graduated from an approved home school program. You must have a valid Social Security number and you cannot have a previous college degree. Pell grants do not have to be repaid but there is only a limited amount of money available for the program and the neediest applicants get priority. Eligibility is based on the total income and expense of the family, the number of people in the family and how many members of the family are trying to attend college. According to one source, most Pell grants are awarded to students from families with incomes of $30,000 or less (Fulciniti, 2015). That is income minus applicable expense. If you are struggling single mom of two kids making less than $30,000 gross, go for it. If you are married and he makes another $30,000, you may not get your grant. It is a conundrum because, if you are married, hopefully he would be able to watch the kids while you attend school. If you aren't married, you can get the grant money but who will watch the kids? The application can be done online and is always worth a shot. Scholarships are available, also, and some organizations target women with children who are trying to better themselves. A web search could match you with the money you need.

There are certificates for being automotive or aircraft mechanics available though technical schools and women can work in those fields. There are construction jobs which begin with minimal class time. One of the most attractive to women is to be an electrician. To wire new construction can be physically demanding but not so much as cement finishing or roofing. It is mostly indoors work and there is an apprenticeship program that could lead to a journeyman position upon the passing of a test (*US News* staff, 2016).

Secretarial work is still necessary and is still the most common job for women in the US. You can usually get a job with only high school courses. The pay may not lucrative, starting about $34,000 per year (Kurtz, 2013). Depending on the company, you may not find a lot of room to move up or you might become a personal assistant and do very well.

Jobs for Working Mothers

I feel sure that one of the reasons why so many women stay secretaries is that the hours do not interfere with mother hood. When couples both work in health care, varying shifts are both a problem and a blessing as it gives them an option of avoiding childcare cost. I have known couples who both work in health care and choose to work alternate shifts. She works days and cares for the children in the evening. He works second shift and cares for the children during the day. It is not ideal but it saves a lot of money in daycare and this situation usually only lasts until the kids get old enough to go to school. When daycare is not an issue, I believe that it is the rare husband who is content to have his wife work the evening shift, forcing him to spend his leisure time at home with the kids. Most men want their wives to be around in the evening for companionship, to make the dinner and help with homework. Secretarial and office work allow for this but often at the cost of a stifled career.

Though health care may offer many jobs, those jobs are not necessarily the most compatible for a working mother. Nurses and technologists seldom begin their careers on day shift. Day shift is a coveted perk and second and third shift employees may wait for years for someone to move or retire from first shift. This is just one of the reasons why so many nurses do not stay in the field. There are wait lists for most nurses' training programs. The interns arrived by the van load at the hospital where I worked. Yet, there is still a nursing shortage and there has been for some time. Nurses are proud to have finished their training. They begin their work with great enthusiasm but often work just long enough to fulfill the commitment that they made when they received their paid internship. By that time, many realize how hard it is. They can be on their feet for long periods. Sometimes they don't get a break. The newer doctors are much more team oriented but there are still some nasty doctors who don't treat them with the respect they deserve. The difficulty of the work, coupled with a shift they can't easily handle with a family results in many women leaving nursing.

Law enforcement is another challenge for the working mom as it is highly unlikely that you will avoid the "off" shifts and, in the event of an emergency, overtime is a given. Who do you have to count on for childcare nights and weekends, possibly for an extended period?

A nursing or medical technology or law enforcement career is possible with young kids but you must find the right employer, who will work with you to find a schedule you can live with. Shifts of ten or twelve hours are sometimes offered to accommodate women who need them. Maybe you have a mother or sister who is willing to let the kids sleep over so that you can work the night shift. That would be an enormous help. Just be aware that, if you are a mother of young children and considering hospital work as a career, best to take off the rose-colored glasses. You are going to need some help. Perhaps your husband does support your choice of career and is willing to watch the kids in the evening while you work second shift, at least until first shift becomes available. Some women work all night, the 11-7 shift or variations thereof. They are home in the evenings with their families. The catch is trying to get any sleep during the day when you have small children to watch.

Numerous websites declare the best jobs for mothers of young children. One such site suggests the obvious, school-teacher. With a few exceptions, you would be off when the kids are off. Your hours would be compatible and teachers do get sick days if the kids are sick. Your children might be in the same school where you are teaching so that you would have that in common. Sounds great, but we can't all be teachers, so what's next?

The same website next offers the job of freelance writer. Do they really expect that you will manage to make a living doing that, a dependable living? I have the same question for their next bright idea, that of fitness instructor. You'd stay in shape but most of the fitness instructors I know are not rolling in money. There is a lot of competition for the client who can pay for personal training. This same website mentions selling Avon or the parties where women buy merchandise. These jobs would be fine if you are just adding gravy to the family meat, but I don't believe you could count on them to pay the mortgage on a long-term basis. Another suggestion is real estate agent (Taylor, 2013). My mother was a real estate agent and I can attest that, if you really want to make a living at it, you must be available when the potential buyer wants to look. That is likely to be weekends and evenings. My mother had to leave the party to show houses on holidays. Again, if you are a mom, you will need someone to take on the kids at a moment's notice.

Pharmacy tech is sometimes recommended for a working mother but we must remember that both pharmacists and pharmacy techs may be expected to work nights now since pharmacies are often open 24 hours. Medical assistant is a popular job. Most doctors don't hire nurses in their practices now. The person who takes your blood pressure and your history is most often a medical assistant. The job usually requires a certificate which can take from one to two years of school and can pay from 22-38 thousand per year.

Working from home sounds like the perfect solution. Those jobs do exist. I know a woman who worked for years from home doing the job of a medical coder. Every test and procedure done for a patient has a code. The code entered decides what the doctor or hospital will be paid so it is important that the code be the right one. There is also a compliance issue. The proper diagnosis code must be entered in order to justify a particular test. A coder gets the dictation from the doctor and enters the proper codes for the tests or procedures he or she has ordered along with the justifiable diagnosis codes. Of course, this takes experience and courses are offered to teach coding but you can make as much as $50,000 per year (Payscale, Human Capital, 2015) and you could do the work at night or whenever the kids would allow so long as you got it done when the doctor or hospital required. However, the information is time sensitive. You won't be able to put it off just because your child has a cold.

Data entry is a job that might be done from home and can pay as much as $30,000 annually. You must be a good typist and be able to persevere with what might prove to be tedious work. Bookkeeping is another option. High school courses are enough to get a job in bookkeeping but it is necessary to know the types of computer software used in bookkeeping today. An experienced bookkeeper can make a little more, perhaps $52,000/yr. (Payscale, Human Capital, 2015).

When I quit my first lab job, primarily because my boss would not keep his hands to himself, I was acutely aware of the need for daycare so I decided that one way for me to make some money would be to keep other women's kids. I ran an in-home daycare for two years, keeping two children at a time, occasionally three, in addition to my child. It was not a lot of money back then and there were no specific laws at that time regulating in-home daycares but, if you like children and have the space, it could be a good income and you might work it into a growing business. Who knows better what a working mother needs in childcare than one who has been there herself?

There are creative jobs to be based at home, such as baking specialty cakes or event planning. The trick is to make a living at it. You will need backup when you transport the cake or have to visit venues to plan a wedding but there are ways to support yourself that don't involve getting up at 5 AM and hauling the kids to daycare. The web design and software development we mentioned can be performed, at least some of the time, at home. Some women have shops in their houses, if they can get the zoning. In-home beauty shops and flower shops work well for working mothers, but you will still need childcare until your kids are of school age. Doing alterations can work out if you have the right sewing machine, the skill and can get enough contracts from area retailers to stay busy. When I called the Company Hot line from our laboratory, because a machine was down, the respondent was usually at home. I could often hear kids in the background. This man or woman did not even have a real instrument in front of them. They had the manual and usually experience with the software and mechanics. I guess that could work for a parent. I personally would not want to be on call and expected to either tell the tech the right thing to do or schedule the service tech, all the while hearing a knock-down drag-out fight between my four- and six-year-olds in my other ear.

Let's face it, most folks are still going to have to go out to work. You might as well make the best money possible while doing it. Many women support families as food servers or bartenders. The only thing to keep in mind, if working in these fields, is that you will be dependent on tips. If you can find a day job where your place of employment is busy and your customers generous, you may be OK. However, the biggest tabs are for dinner and drinks in the evening.

The worst jobs, I believe, for working mothers are the ones working as sales staff in retail stores that are open all hours. Wal-Mart and Home Depot will move you all over the schedule and, unless you have reliable on call childcare or you can make a pact with your boss to keep your hours stable, a single mom with small kids won't last in these places.

Some women work in construction, even on highways. They work in factories, bakeries, and grocery stores. All these jobs are valuable and, if they fit your needs, good for you. If they don't, what can you do? You can learn to do something that will pay your bills and, if you are supporting or co-supporting children, the hours must be doable. If you find yourself working as a waitress or a grocery cashier and it isn't covering expenses, try to take some courses in the evenings. Continuing education courses are given at many high schools at minimum cost. It will be hard when you already have so much responsibility, but you will be proud of yourself that you did it, and what's even better, your children will be proud of you, too.

You Have To Get the Job First

So now you've decided on a job you want to do. You apply. Most applications are online now so you may not have the opportunity to expand on your qualifications and experience until the interview. Then you get the call! Smile and Groan. An interview can be scary. Once you are established in a particular field, you won't find the interview so onerous. I didn't even formally interview for my last few jobs. Every hospital had someone who had worked with me or for me, and that person was willing to vouch for me, so getting hired was easy. However, it wasn't easy at first and it probably won't be easy for you, either. There is a glut of advice on how to interview successfully. Of course, you know to dress professionally, to be well groomed and only very lightly perfumed if at all. Don't be late. Don't chitchat in the waiting room with other applicants about how nervous you are or how you are worried about your qualifications. There are people who will use it against you in their own interviews. These are basic. However, there are things you might not immediately recognize as skewing your chances at getting the job.

Don't cross your arms during the interview. It gives the message that you are a "closed" sort of person, or crossed arms can be interpreted as disagreement with what is being said to you. Don't be distracted by your phone or your bracelet. Fidgeting suggests that your attention is elsewhere. Don't claim to have skills which you do not have, but be sure to mention it if you have a similar skill and say that you are sure you could learn what's necessary. Perhaps most important, familiarize yourself with the company for which you are applying. Look them up on the internet; pull up the names of their officers. Are any of them women? What is their market, what kind of customers are they concerned with (if applicable)? Ask pertinent questions at your interview about what they do and how you can help their growth. It is difficult to refrain from asking about salary, but the general consensus is that you should wait until you are offered the job. You can always say no if the amount offered is not enough.

And it must be enough. Julie King points out that employers can't be blamed if women are willing to take less and to give in too soon in salary negotiation. Of course, they will low-ball you (King J. A., 1995). It is up to you to research the internet before you go. Find out what the going rate is for the job you are offered. If you have no previous experience, you may have to take the low end of the range, but, please, don't take the low figure even if you do have experience with the idea that you will work hard and you will make up the difference by being rewarded with generous raises. In a perfect world, maybe. The real fact is, you will be pegged as a person who will work for less and still work harder than those who asked for more. They will get the more and you will get the work. If you need to state a figure that you want during an interview and you have done your homework, state the higher side of the range you got from your research. You can expect the hiring person to talk you down but their figure will likely still be more than if you state the minimum. Also, find out what benefits the company offers. They may be mentioned on their website. Government jobs may not pay as highly but they offer great benefits and pension plans. That is a tax-free savings plan for you, security for the future. To ask the cost of health insurance, how much vacation you would get or what other perks are available might be seen as presumptuous in an interview but are fair questions if you get an offer and are negotiating salary.

One reason given for the fact that women typically accept less money in salary negotiations is that men and women feel differently about money. A survey done by Maddy Dychtwald and associates found that to men, money is freedom. To women it is security (Dychtwald, 2010). I think that is true. Our first thought is the security of our families and we tell ourselves, "This amount will be enough. If I ask for more, I might not get the job?" If you think this way, it will carry over into asking for raises. Inform yourself as to what the going rate is and don't talk yourself into taking less.

Yes, you can take less at hiring and hope to take your complaint to the EEOC if you find, down the line, that you are not being paid commensurate with a man. However, in May of 2015, the EEOC had a backlog of 70,000 pending charges of workplace discrimination (Wolf, 2015). Better get that fair wage up front.

One thing to remember is not to trash you current or previous employer. After all, you took their money and it won't sound good if you volunteer to the new company all the dirty laundry of the old. The interviewer will fear you might do the same to them in the future. You may have to state your previous salary on your application. If the new company tries to match it, in the hope that you will take the same wage, say that one reason you left or are planning to leave is to better yourself. There is nothing wrong with asking the interviewer what kind of person they are looking for or what kind of person fits in best but don't do that at the start of the interview, maybe in the middle. It will give you an idea about which of your skills to highlight.

In the lab, it was customary for several people to participate in an interview of a possible new employee, the lead techs for the shift needing a tech and/or the supervisor of the lab. Having to deal with more than one person may seem daunting but it can work in your favor. If three people interview you and two are on the fence but one is enthusiastic, that third person can convince the others to give you a chance. You are bound to have better chemistry with one or another of a group.

Employers are legally constrained from asking you whether you are married, whether you have or are planning to have children or even how old you are. However, they get around some of these laws by asking for your driver's license, which has your birth date or asking you to have coffee and then steering the conversation around to family matters and hoping you will volunteer information about your family situation. Don't do it if you can help it. You may know that you have adequate childcare and that you will be a perfectly reliable employee but, if the other candidate is childless and you both have equal qualifications, she may get the job simply because they don't want to take a chance on absence due to family problems. If the interviewer backs you into a corner and you feel that you will come off as secretive if you don't mention your family, then say, I have two kids but I also have great childcare and it will not interfere with my work for you.

Likewise, in a job interview, don't say that you really want this particular job because it fits in so well with your children's school hours. That may be the case but this potential employer wants you to concentrate on company goals or, at least, pretend to. At this point, you are not a mother or a wife. You must convince this interviewer that you will be good for this company. Whether it is good for you is immaterial to them.

Alternately, you can't come on too strong. You might be tempted to say, "You know, I deserve this job. I've worked for twenty years and been passed over before. There is no reason you should not hire me." You may feel this is true and maybe it is but we all know that a man who says this may come off as confident. A woman making the same statement may be perceived as strident.

Try not to be too scared at the interview. Management wants to hire the right person. Most employers will go to great lengths to make a new hire work out. They have expended a lot of money and time to advertise, interview and train. If you don't stay, they have to do it all over again. If you interview and you don't get the job, there will be others. Sometimes, a company is required to advertise a position even though they have already privately decided on a person they want to hire. They go through the motions but you never really have a chance. Even if you sense that his might be the case, put yourself out there anyway. Other jobs will come up and they may remember you. Don't make light of your accomplishments. If you haven't worked outside the home in years, don't say, "Well, I really haven't done anything in a long time." This is not the time for self-deprecation. Look for accomplishments. If you organized a carpool with several other mothers, speak up. That is an organizing process. You may be asked in the interview one of the stock questions, "Tell me about a situation where you had to deal with a difficult person." If you had a mother in the carpool who did not pull her weight, who called off and put more stress on the other mothers, how did you handle that? If you just took the extra driving yourself, you need to learn management. If you told her she would have to do equal driving or her kids would not be in the pool, say so. Confidence is an absolute must, so, if necessary, fake it until you feel it.

You will be asked, in most cases, to list your skills. Whatever you do, don't leave blank spaces. If you weren't in the military, of course, that gets an NA, but if you can type (possibly not well, but you know how), put it down. If you sold Girl Scout cookies, that is marketing. You have to sell yourself. Doing that on an application online is easier than in person. I hate it when an interviewer says, "What are your strengths and weaknesses," and that is a stock question. You may have your strengths on the tip of your tongue but, if you say you don't have any weaknesses, you come off as conceited and if you admit to some, you may skew your interview.

I cannot stress enough the importance of networking when both looking for and interviewing for a job. If you know someone, even tangentially, who works in a company that you might like to work for, invite her to go for coffee or lunch. Find out the strengths and weaknesses of this possible place of employment in the opinion of someone who should know. If your contact has a positive outlook on her employer and is in good standing, ask whether you can mention her in your interview or list her as a reference. If she hates the place, ask why. Sometimes it is personal but sometimes it is just a toxic place. Now is the time to learn that fact, not after you are hired.

There are signs of the toxic workplace. I have worked in one of those, a clinic, and, if I had followed my instincts, I wouldn't have accepted the job. First of all, the office help seemed stressed, dashing around like they had lost something important. I soon found out why there was always such upheaval. My job was not only to supervise the small lab but also to order for it. My employers were a married couple, the primary doctor and his wife. He wanted his supplies pronto, no excuses. She, however, wanted to get the best price and would use up time haggling with different vendors before she would assign a PO so that I could actually make the purchase. Of course, we would run out of tissues and other supplies, and I would get the blame, though the orders would have been filled on time if the requests had gone through promptly. This same problem hampered purchases in all the departments. In addition, if there was blame to be laid for any error involving the wife, she was very quick to lay it on an underling and the doctor did not really care whether the object of his very visible wrath was guilty or not. The techs running the lab, though well intentioned, were woefully under trained and Quality Control was practically non-existent. I stayed long enough to show them what a real QC program was, and then I escaped. After that, I paid attention to the "vibe" present in any organization before I committed myself to it.

One of the attitudes mentioned over and over again in literature is enthusiasm. Women show enthusiasm better than men and companies like that in their hiring practices. If you don't feel enthusiastic about a company, it is going to be hard to fake it, so try to find a job that you think is offering you something of value besides a paycheck. A full-time job will take up more than a third of your life. Find something to like about it.

Whatever job you get, you are going to have to get raises or the rise in the cost of loving will shortly outstrip your wages. One suggestion for arming yourself when asking for a rise is to have proof of success. When someone gives you a compliment or thanks you for helping them with a problem, get it in writing. If it's in an e-mail, print it out. If it's verbal, ask them to e-mail it to you (Dempsay, Rachel and Williams, Joan C., 2014). Tell them why. They will understand. Keep a file and have it with you when you ask to see the boss. It is bound to give you a boost.

Going Back to Work in a New Field, Motherhood

We've already said that corporate America has resisted making a place in the job world for working mothers. All of us who became pregnant while working have had to make the decision, When do I tell my boss? What will he say? Most of us waited until we couldn't hide it anymore because we assumed our impending absence would be met with groans. We all tried to keep a stiff upper lip if we didn't feel well while pregnant because, while a male colleague recovering from a heart attack would be pampered and asked to take it easy, we all felt that pregnancy was a choice and, therefore, we needn't expect any slack. We made it hard for ourselves and for the pregnant women who came after us because we felt we had no protection and did not want to lose our jobs. One source suggests asking the boss's secretary what kind of mood he is in before we tell him the good news. Please! Why are we apologizing for bringing life into the world?

Of course, we have to be considerate. If your job is going to be shared between co-workers while you are on maternity leave, bring them up to date and keep them that way. Write down the tasks you are currently undertaking. Get it straight with your boss or with HR about how much time you are actually allowed to take off. Most places require you to use your paid time off and that time off may be included in the twelve weeks maternity leave, not added to it.

Then the baby comes. In our minds, we feel that we will just manage somehow, juggling a baby with our job. We feel the same commitment to our career, but we now have another commitment. It is hard for women who work defined hours to arrange childcare and "get it all done" in the time allowed. It's worse if your hours vary. Even professional women struggle. In their book *Everything a Working Mother Needs to Know*, Anne Weisberg and Carol Buckler, attorneys both, tell about a fellow professional, a senior vice president of a Fortune 500 company, who arrived at the babysitter's house one morning to find nobody home. She eventually found another sitter but she was, by then, two hours late to work. Instead of telling her boss the real situation, she told the office that she had a flat tire (Buckler, Carol A. and Weisberg, Anne C., 1994). It is more acceptable in our work world to have a flat tire, which could happen to anyone, than to have a babysitter problem which happens only to working parents. I do say parents plural, because two people had this child and I do believe that, had the father been met with the same dilemma, he would also have used the excuse because he, too, would not want to be singled out as less committed because he has a child.

Why is it like this? It is very possible to do a great job while having children. One mother in Weisberg and Buckler's book tells how she did it. She did not take coffee breaks, she didn't take long lunches and she might work while lunching; she didn't shop. She took work home because she knew she had to leave by 5 PM. Bully for her that she managed. Work–life problem solved. However, I'm not sure it's so easy to organize the other issues of household and family when you get home.

We are still not seeing the forest. It is impossible to be all things to all people. Working mothers must be willing to acknowledge that they can't have gleaming floors, homemade cookies, svelte bodies toned at the gym, adorable well-behaved children and dynamic careers all at the same time without a great deal of effort, strategy and probably stress. When you go back to work, solicit the advice and camaraderie of other working mothers. Tell your husband you cannot do it alone. Ignore the floor commercials. You don't eat off the floor, and if the kids do, it will bolster their immune systems.

CHAPTER 8. HARASSMENT; SEXUAL AND OTHERWISE

There are many facets to a good job. The work may be something you enjoy. The pay and the benefits may be all you could wish but the people with whom you work, the culture of the workplace will most often be the factor that keeps you on the job or drives you away from it. Sometimes, as I've mentioned, there are warning signs before you start that all will not be well on a new job. However, other times, especially as companies seek to hire for diversity, they will hire a new person, quite possibly a woman, into a work culture that will see a woman who is not only unwelcome but also is a convenient target. You may find yourself in the lion's den.

I well remember the bad old days before the laws went into place regarding sexual harassment in the workplace. All of my friends who came of age in the 60s remember them, too. Sexual harassment still exists, of course, but it was rampant back then, far more prevalent in 1968 when I began work in the lab. There were beds in the halls at that time as the hospital was overfull. I worked my way through my initial laboratory training running EKGs and washing glassware. I would go the patient's bedside in the hall and pull the curtains around myself and the patient for privacy. My supervisor at the time came up behind me, while I was in the midst of the EKG, and put his arms around me through the curtains, pulling me to him in no uncertain way. This kind of behavior was common but nonetheless unwelcome. One of his most obnoxious tricks, which I had seen him do to others, was to wait until the tech (we were all women) was at the microscope, then wrap himself around her from behind, pinning her between himself and the bench, squeezing her breasts with his arms. When he did it to me, I gave him an elbow in the ribs as hard as I could and his attitude toward me became more circumspect, though resentful. I finally finished my training elsewhere, as he was all-powerful and a woman at that time either put up with bad treatment or she left.

Sometimes, the infringement on your person is not overt, but rather an effort to make you uneasy and distract you from your job. Jean, one year my senior, tells of her experience in the 1970s, just when the term "sexual harassment" had been coined and word of it had begun to spread. She was doing an inspection of a business. The manager of the business led her to an upstairs office for the closing conference. His desk was at the end of a large empty room, distant from other workers. In Jean's words, "He told me to use his chair, which was behind the desk and he sat in the other chair which was between me and the door. As I was going over my findings with him, I suddenly got the feeling he wasn't really paying attention to what I was saying but had focused on me. He didn't say anything but just the way he was watching me made me leery, so I gathered my paperwork together and as I stood up I showed him a particular paragraph in one of the publications I was leaving for him. By doing this I had distracted him enough to be able to say something like, 'If you don't have any further questions I'll be on my way.' Then I quickly headed out of the room and downstairs." Perhaps the manager sought to rattle Jean, or perhaps worse. We've all experienced the creepy feeling she describes and most of us have had a manager or other male try to intimidate us.

That was over forty years ago. Yet, just this month *The New York Times* reported that the dean of the law school at Berkeley was accused of sexual harassment of his executive assistant over a six-month period of time. He hugged and kissed her repeatedly though she resisted and complained to supervisors. She finally sent a letter to Human Resources. Berkeley did have a policy in place to deal with sexual harassment and an investigation found the dean to be guilty of the allegations. Yet he was not dismissed, and it was only after the plaintiff initiated a lawsuit that he finally stepped down — not permanently, but as a leave of absence (Hartocollis, 2016). This took place in a law school of great renown. How hard do you suppose it is for a low-wage worker, who perhaps does not have English as a first language, to satisfactorily report sexual misconduct by a superior and expect appropriate action?

While we have the government to petition when all other avenues for redress fail, the government, too, has condoned sexual misconduct by employees by ignoring repeated complaints. Some National Park Service Boatmen, responsible for the raft trips through the Grand Canyon, have been guilty of soliciting unwanted sex from female co-workers for 10 to 15 years. One female employee reported having a camera shoved up her dress. Off color jokes and sexual innuendo were common. When female co-workers refused the advances, the women were disciplined or even refused food. A supervisor of the guides was temporarily suspended in 2005 for grabbing the crotch of an employee. Yet, it was not until thirteen women filed a formal complaint that attention was finally paid. Even so, the supervisor was allowed to retire in 2015. Both the boatmen who had groped and propositioned a co-worker and the one who took the picture under the woman's dress were allowed to resign. The third boatman had not yet been disciplined as of January 2016. A human resources employee remarked that the park was a "good ol' boy network" (Kaplan, 2016). Is that supposed to be some kind of excuse? It seems that good ol' boy is synonymous with bully. Today it was reported that the Park Service's solution to the problem has been to dissolve the unit involved in river trips. The running of future trips, including the hiring of boatmen, will be contracted out, removing the government from having to discipline its own (Associated Press, 2016).

Many of the women who support the effort against domestic and sexual violence have experienced it themselves. One story came from an ex-military woman who was assaulted by her commanding officer while out on maneuvers. I'm sure he had done it before and I'm also sure he thought she would never tell;

but she did tell. She lived through a period of misery as even the men with whom she had served, and who she thought were her friends, turned their backs. The man's superiors were obliged to follow up on her complaint, but they didn't like it. This gutsy lady had to keep demanding her rights until the powers that be finally administered a lie detector test to the perpetrator and the man failed it, after which he admitted his guilt. He was very close to drawing his pension but he lost it and left the service under a cloud. She scored one small victory but didn't sign up for another tour of duty. Her record would have followed her and she felt that the male establishment would have punished her for her bravery in any unit in which she served.

Sometimes, there is just one problem male, one guy who delights in telling off-color jokes or making remarks about your appearance that you could do without. Sometimes he encourages others guys to join in. They may be testing you. It's a tough position. If you go to HR and make a big deal out of it, you are pegged as a troublemaker. If you don't, it will likely get worse. One option is to take the high road. Ask them to think about what they just said and whether that is how they were raised to talk to women. It won't help the hard-core abuser, but it might stop the show-offs. Psychologists tell us that most men who threaten your personal space or body are not sociopaths as such. They are carrying out the mandates of the culture in which they were raised. To refuse to bully and objectify women, if that is the prevailing culture, will make a man look like a coward in the eyes of his like-minded buddies. Testosterone is the hormone responsible for both sex and violence and our society is rife with violence, be it in the form of blind patriotism, the collecting of firearms and knives (both weapons of penetration), bloody and brutal sports and, of course, video games that reward killing and maiming. Young males get mixed messages. Male anatomy may make them bigger and stronger but society and the law have ordained that, just because you can push women around, doesn't mean you are allowed to do so (Spencer, 2014).

We might expect that the ultra-feminine women would be most likely to be harassed by men as sexual objects but research shows this not to be the case. It is often the women who demonstrate more masculine traits, not nurturing, not gentle, not willing to take a backseat, that receive the most diligent sexual offenses. It is as though she is being abused because she does not fit the female stereotype that exists in the minds of her tormentors (Dempsay, Rachel and Williams, Joan C., 2014). Whatever your type, it is important that you ooze confidence. The sexual predator will leap on any prey he considers weak. Stand up and speak with assurance. I do know that is easier said than done, but even if they laugh, it is better than cringing. If you are thinking of bringing suit, be aware that the harassment has to be clear-cut before the government will take an interest. It the abuser is your supervisor and he makes it plain that you will get nowhere in your job unless he gets the attention he wants, get what proof you can. If he's dumb enough to e-mail his suggestions, print and save them. If he's done it before, get testimony. The other kind of harassment is general, where the walls are full of pornographic pictures and every day brings new lewd remarks. I would take pictures of the pornography and take this to the supervisor first. If he's one of them, you have a decision to make. Some women could take it in stride and hope the taunts will subside as she proves her worth on the job. The important thing is that you do have redress if you choose to use it. One thing to remember is not to use company computers if you are documenting instances of abuse or communicating with legal entities about your experiences. Any document written or stored on a company server belongs to them and you will certainly be giving them advance notice if you make this kind of information available to your superiors because they have access to the documents at work.

There are other kinds of harassment. It can come from co-workers of either sex or from a female boss. I worked for a woman who "managed" those under her by trying to pit them against each other. She is still working so I'll do her the favor of not using her real name. We'll call her Brenda. Brenda was not a hands-on supervisor. She seldom entered the department and knew little of the day-to-day operation. When it came time for Performance Evaluations, every tech reported the same kind of experience. Brenda would rattle on at length about some other tech and the problems she was having with him or her. She never really got around to discussing your performance or lack thereof. It was immaterial, as she always gave the absolute minimum raise. Her value to the company was to keep labor costs down. I was never sure if she thought that running some other tech down in my presence was her way of trying to make me feel good about my own performance or just her way of venting, perhaps against someone who had stood up to her. Either way, she was a terrible supervisor. We all knew what she was doing. We knew that any of us could be fair game for her acid tongue. She invited confidences, giving you every opportunity to agree with her poor assessment of the tech she was vilifying. Woe to the person who fell into this trap, as she was sure to go to that tech and tell him or her exactly what you had said, leaving out her complicity. We knew better than to expect her to be a champion for our department. Whatever request came in, we were expected to meet it, no matter how unreasonable. We also knew that it would do us little good to go over her head, which some had tried. She could be nasty and always held a grudge. Fortunately, since we were almost all experienced techs and we saw little of her, we managed ourselves. Because of her, however, we did it with little hope of recompense, just for love of the work and for each other.

In *Working for Bitches*, Meredith Fuller outlines several kinds of bad female supervisors. I don't think it's necessary to give each kind a title, as they can and do overlap. However, Ms. Fuller does a good job of describing the kind of behavior you may need to watch out for. With a boss like Brenda, you disappear once you have left her office. You are only valuable for what you can do for her. I'm sure this is true of male bosses, also, but it is even more galling in a Sister.

Both sexes can be bullies, but I think women are more devious in their tactics. Female bullies are likely to target only certain people, specifically those they think are powerless. They manipulate by excluding. They leave your name out of an e-mail, then, after you miss the meeting, they claim it was an oversight. They dismiss your suggestions, though the same offering might meet with approval when it comes from another employee. When you ask to speak with her, she is always too busy (Fuller, 2013). I wish I could tell you how to work with this type of boss, but the solution is probably to ask for a transfer. You can bet that you won't be the first to have done so.

There is the micro-manager, who feels that she must be included in every discussion and decision, though that may seriously slow down the process. She never feels her staff works as hard as she does or takes the work seriously enough. She may try to show you up in meetings. Ms. Fuller calls her The Insecure.

I have seen the kind of boss who refuses to promote or transfer because that means they will have to train a new person for the job. Either, they don't want to take the trouble to advertise and hire or they just can't stand to see anyone else get ahead. With this kind of boss, the employee usually winds up going to another company because, HR will not place her in the new position until her present supervisor lets her go. It is a no win situation for the employee. This kind of boss is angry when you find another job on your own. They take no responsibility for their delaying tactics.

The problem woman in your life doesn't have to be a boss. My friend tells of his brief tenure as a production chief, supervising women. This was many years ago and the competition for attention and approval was fierce. Cat fights were common. Competition among women can still be fierce but I believe it was worse when women had so few outlets for their ambition. I've seen the same kind of dog eat dog attitude among PTA members. When women do not work outside the home or their job allows very little opportunity to stand out, they try to do so by besting other women. Some of their tactics are downright snarky, complimenting an action or a feature of your appearance to your face and laughing at you behind your back. If this kind of women thinks you may have a better chance for promotion, she will do anything in her power to see that you don't get it. She may not get it, either, but it keeps you in what she considers to be your place. This kind of infighting is counterproductive. Women are already at a disadvantage for getting promotions, for breaking the glass ceiling, for being taken seriously. When we destroy what bonds we have with one another, we become one against the many, not many against the many.

The bases for conflict are as many as there are people but one that comes up is the feminine vs. the more masculine mode of interaction with those around and above you. The feminine personality believes in using her femininity, not in a flirtatious way, but to get what she wants by smiling, being attractive, asking nicely, explaining herself and relying on the good nature of those above her to reward her efforts. The more masculine type of women expects good work and demands it. She tries to treat others fairly but cares little for window dressing and will not suck up to those above her to get what she's asking when she feels strongly that it is the right thing to do and that others are depending on her to make things happen (Dempsay, Rachel and Williams, Joan C., 2014). I have worked for both types of women and I know that, as a manager, I was more the masculine type. I don't have the patience for the kind of finesse it takes to use feminine wiles and then wait for the grantor to come around to your way of thinking. However, in the health care consortium in which I worked, many of the laboratory department heads were attractive women. They were no doubt competent in their fields but it was noticeable that upper management, mostly male, preferred to hire the feminine personality type if they had to deal with females.

I was fortunate in that I worked in an industry, which was comprised of mostly women. One tech I worked with birthed four children while on the same job. We made allowances. Many sources demonstrate that this is the exception, not the rule. In many jobs, when the employee returns from maternity leave, she is relegated to some desk job that she had outgrown years before. One source describes her frustration, saying, "I had a baby, not a lobotomy." The same source talks about a law firm where partners decline to use an associate because "she has four kids at home" (Dempsay, Rachel and Williams, Joan C., 2014). The tech with whom I worked adjusted her hours to allow her to take and pick up children. She made arrangements as they became necessary. She was one of the best and most knowledgeable techs I ever had the privilege to know, and I am sure the lawyer those partners chose to exclude was just as able to deal with her family. After all, do fathers with four children get excluded because of their family? Perhaps their wives work. Perhaps they are even single fathers. The fact is, that they do not run into the same doubts and quandaries when it comes to being hired or to being utilized to the fullest extent because they have children. This quibbling over whether or not you can still do your job after you become a mother is another kind of harassment.

There is a second kind of grief that is doled out to women with children, especially as they go on maternity leave. There was one tech in my hospital who complained bitterly about have to take an extra weekend once during the entire twelve weeks of another tech's maternity leave or having to cover a department she did not like because we were one tech short due to maternity leave. This tech had no children and did not have any patience with those who did. The rest of us tried to counter this negative attitude by reminding the complaining tech of what a good tech the new mother was. We stressed how she never asked for undue concessions and how hard it would make our jobs, at least temporarily, if she suddenly decided not to come back at all. Sticking up for your sister is a must, if that kind of conflict is not to fester and grow. I'm sure, had we worked in a place where there were more techs like the complainer, harassment due to motherhood would have been a larger problem.

I found it reassuring to read that only 55 percent of women report conflict with other women to be a problem in their jobs: mothers vs. non-mothers, feminine vs. more masculine, part-time vs. full-time. That means that if you are suffering this kind of work environment, it does not exist everywhere (Dempsay, Rachel and Williams, Joan C., 2014).

Conflicts can emerge as to management styles. I was raised in the era of authoritarianism. My boss gave an order and we all scrambled to carry it out. The largest group of workers in the US today is that of the Millennials, born between 1981 and 1997. Their expectation of work is much different. They were educated using workgroups and they learned early to be able to compete as a group. Their management style is more team based. They are more likely to listen to the ideas of others and find it hard to deal with someone who wants to manage them in the old way (McCleary, 2016). They are far more likely to use technology and have been instrumental in forcing the use of mobile banking. They are more likely to think globally, forcing fast food chains to use more healthful ingredients and to use their power to exert influence such as in the management of Toms Shoes, which gives away a pair of shoes to a child in need with each purchase (Andrews, 2016). Of course, there are going to be conflicts between the old and the new guard. Millennials may feel that they should be free to go to Yoga in the middle the day and work an hour later to make up for the absence. A boss of my era is thinking, "What?" Sixty percent of Millennials report that they expect to hear from their managers at least once a day. They expect feedback and kudos (McCleary, 2016). Remember, this is the generation who had cap and gown graduations from nursery school. A worker of this generation may see hard-line management, a dressing down in a meeting or a failure to respond to a suggestion as harassment. Millennials expect to change jobs often. If you don't want to constantly be training replacements, it's best to learn to manage new workers in the new way.

Chapter 9. Income Tax — The Single Bracket Racket

We are going to leave Mary and Susan now and talk about the working woman who makes a better income. Let us talk now about a single mother (she doesn't have to be a mother) who is an experienced RN. The mean annual salary for a Registered Nurse in Florida is $63,287 but let's take the situation of an advanced nurse who has taken extra courses and probably shoulders extra responsibility. Let's say she makes the upper end of the usual pay scale, which is $80,000 (Payscale, Human Capital, 2016). We will call our RN Jennie. Jennie is single with two children. She uses the standard deduction amount when she files her income tax since she has not yet bought a house and does not have enough deductions to benefit from itemizing. After taking the standard deduction and her three exemptions, her adjusted income is $59,050. According to the tax table, Jennie will pay a tax of $9,079 as Head of Household. If she did not have children, she would pay $10,550. If we look at the middle of the table, we see what a pair of married taxpayers, filing jointly, would pay, on the same income, just $8,074.

Now think about this. It is the same amount of money. Why are two people allowed to pay as much as $2,476 less in taxes than the single person? Two people in the married household are using the roads, being protected by the military, enjoying all the benefits paid for in taxes but are paying considerably less for these privileges. It is reminiscent of the Social Security discrepancy. Maybe, the income from the married couple is a combination of two people's pay but it can just as likely be from only one spouse who is paying into the tax base while the other partner did not contribute any wages at all. It makes no difference to the tax law. A single working woman is obliged to file either in the single category or as Head of Household, and either one is going to cost her more than her married sister who may not work at all.

The difference in tax obligation is not noticeable in the lowest brackets but it doesn't take long to show up. At a taxable income of $20,000, a single person pays $2,543, a head of household pays $2,346 and the married couple (even if there is only one wage earner) pays $2,081. That's $265 less than the head of household, and the head of household is supporting children or other qualifying persons. That's what "Head of Household" means.

The higher the wages, the higher the discrepancy becomes. If our nurse becomes a Nurse Practitioner or other high paying specialty and starts earning $100,000/year, she may pay income tax on $75,000. Her tax obligation, at that stage, will be $13,079 as a Head of Household. If she were married and he did not work at all, she would only be liable for $10,344 (IRS, 2015). That is a reduction in tax of $2,735, although two adults and their children would be getting more benefit from all the things our taxes pay for. Once again, the working woman (or man) is paying for the one who does not work.

There is a penalty of sorts for being single and having a child or children. In 2016, the Earned Income Tax Credit phases out for a single taxpayer or for a Head of Household parent with two children at a taxable income of $44.648. A married couple, filing jointly, could make $50,198 and still get the credit, though only one of them worked.

One might assume that the tax law was trying to encourage "family values" and reward people for getting married, but marriage can be a detriment, too, tax-wise. There is such a thing as a "marriage penalty," and that kicks in when both people work. High income married couples can pay a large penalty due to the tax brackets for married couples and the fact that, after $250,000, a Medicare sur-tax kicks in (Pomerleau, 2015). You may not feel too sorry for this couple earning $300,000, but they are both working and paying tax. Neither of them is benefitting without paying.

A couple making much less can also be hurt by the marriage penalty. Take two people with one child, who each make only $15,000. They would pay a higher tax bill as a married couple than they would as unmarrieds. This is because the single parent who claimed the child would qualify for Head of Household and be able to use the higher standard deduction. That parent would also be eligible for a higher Earned Income Tax Credit. Their total marriage penalty is $1,087.88. (Pomerleau, 2015).

There is also such a thing as a "marriage bonus," which comes into play when two people of disparate incomes marry. If one makes $50,000 and the other makes $25,000, their combined tax bill will be less than if they were unmarried, due to the wider tax brackets for married couples (Pomerleau, 2015).

The point here is not whether all married people save money in taxes by virtue of being married. It is, rather, that single people tend not to benefit in the same way if they strive to get ahead, make higher wages or work more hours. The tax law is illogical as well as far too complicated.

CHAPTER 10. WHO'S BEING SQUEEZED IN THE SANDWICH
GENERATION?

The first time I heard the term "sandwich generation" was
from a female pathologist with whom I worked in Gainesville,
Florida. I commented one day that she looked tired. She replied,
"Well, I'm of the sandwich generation, squeezed between my
teenage children and my aging parents." This was from a doctor, a specialist, who probably waited to have her children until
her education was complete. Now the adolescent children were
pushing the envelope at the same time that her parents also
needed her attention.

In 2005, the CDC estimated that 21% of US households were
impacted by care-giving responsibilities beyond the immediate family and 90% of those caregivers were unpaid. The CDC
goes on to say that the typical caregiver is a 46-year-old woman
with some college experience who devotes more than 20 hours
per week to the care of her mother (Center for Disease Control,
2011). The care these women give their relatives is saving the
American taxpayer a bundle as otherwise Medicare or Medicaid
would likely be picking up the bill to have professionals do it.

The bread of the sandwich may vary. Some working women
are caring for grandchildren at least part of the time and, in our
society today, often full time. About 2.7 million grandparents are

primary caregivers for their grandchildren under the age of 18. That was not always the case. In 1970, about 3% of all American children lived in grandparent-maintained homes. Today it is closer to 6%. The reasons given for this change include teen pregnancy, divorce, drug use and incarceration (Ellis, Renee R. and Simmons,Tavia, 2014). Working women caring for grandchildren contend with the same daycare problems as other working women. Working women caring for disabled children or grandchildren face even greater challenges.

Some caretakers for the disabled are quite up in age. If the parent or grandparent is retired or disabled, but still the legal caregiver, Social Security will pay a Disabled Child Benefit for the child or grandchild. There is also a death benefit if the caretaker dies. The benefit is based on the Social Security earnings record of the care-giving adult. This benefit is termed SSDI, Social Security Disability Income. As you might imagine, being responsible for a disabled child affects the caregiver's ability to make a good living and to pay commensurately into the Social Security system, especially if the child remains disabled as a chronological adult. In many instances, the disability of a child prevents the caregiver from working at all.

If the caregiver does not have enough quarters invested in Social Security to qualify for the disability benefit for his or her child, the disabled child may be eligible for a different benefit called SSI, Supplemental Security Income. SSI differs from Social Security in that it is not funded from Social Security taxes. The money paid to beneficiaries of Supplemental Social Security comes from general revenue; that is income tax. There are strict limits to what a beneficiary of SSI may own or have in the bank (SSI, SSDI, 2015). This can create a quandary for the caregiver of a disabled child, whether that child is a disabled adult or a minor.

Janey has some money in the bank and a retirement plan but she can no longer work due to having to care for her disabled daughter. As her severely affected Down's child was born early in her working career, Janey had not put in the required 40 quarters (ten years, not necessarily consecutive) to qualify for SSDI for her daughter. Janey's husband found dealing with the medical and physical requirements of parenting a challenged child to be more than he had bargained for; he has disappeared from the lists of the employed as well as from her address book. In order for her daughter to qualify for SSI, Janey must rid herself of any assets beyond a home, a car and $2000 in the bank. She will forever remain dependent on the government for help as ordinary daycare is not sufficient and skilled nursing care costs more that Janey could ever hope to make in any job for which she is qualified. We can only hope that Janey has some relative who can provide her with respite care because, as the child grows older and heavier, the feeding, lifting and transport to frequent doctor's appointments will wear on Janey's health.

This is chronic care giving as opposed to acute. A healthy child gets a virus and her mom can expect to be up for a few nights, to worry if the fever seems to last too long, to clean up spills and vomit. But she will only do this for a week or so. Janey will do it for as long as she or the child lives. As for the people who resent the money Janey gets from SSI, shame on them.

Women also care for infirm parents. Some women care for children or grandchildren as well as infirm parents and they are likely to be lower income women with the least help and the least recognition. Jennifer Johnson in her book *Getting By On the Minimum* points out that working class women who are involved in the lives of relatives work under enormous stress. They are often struggling to raise teens in areas where teens are likely to go astray, trying to give younger children or grandchildren enough attention and, in addition, are called upon to deal with ailing parents who need to be kept safe and cared for. This mother/grandmother does all this after a physically exhausting day and with not enough money to make it all come right (Johnson, 2002).

My daughter had two boys and when they were young and one would fall ill, I helped her care for them. It was a relay race. I got up early after my second shift job and drove an hour to her home, where I watched the child while she worked her day job. She would skip lunch to be home by 1:30 PM so that I could leave for my job in time to arrive at work an hour later. Sometimes this went on for several days. Of course, I loved my grandsons and my daughter, but the fact remains that we both got very tired.

I read recently an article about Jill Abramson, former executive editor of *the New York Times* and the first female to hold that position. Jill Abramson teaches at Harvard University. She writes a political column for *The Guardian* and is authoring a book about the future of journalism. In addition, Jill participates in speaking engagements and interviews. Yet, during the school year, she lives with her surgeon daughter and the daughter's surgeon husband as an "extra pair of hands" to help with her granddaughter (Griffin, 2016). No matter your status, no matter your economic bracket, women take care of their own and fit the rest of their lives around it.

A more onerous kind of care giving involves the aging parents. At first thought, you might believe that this would be quite like childcare but that would be wrong. Elders are adults. They may be deranged, confused, unreasonable adults, but they are still adults and they expect to be treated as such. They especially expect it from a daughter they raised. I say daughter because, seven out of ten times, it is the female child who is left with the responsibility for mom or dad. In the days before women worked outside the home, it was expected because the son was working. Daughter is working, now, too, but society still expects her to take on the care giving. Men simply do not anticipate this eventuality.

When our own mother was dying, all three of her children and their families got together for her May birthday. Mother's Day occurred one week later and I again asked my brother to bring his family down for the event. He lived about forty-five minutes away and reminded me that he "was just down there." I told him frankly that it was Mom's last Mother's Day. Despite her wasted condition, he did not believe her death was imminent. Though it stared him in the face, he could not foresee a time when his mother would no longer be there. I can say that he and his family did come for Mother's Day, and our mother died five weeks later.

Elder care is different, too, because children will gradually become responsible for themselves. They will eventually become independent. Not so with mom or dad, who may have physical infirmities that will only become more disabling or, even worse, they may develop mental declines like dementia. Most times, we cannot expect a happy conclusion. When a parent's illness is first diagnosed, it reverberates through the whole family. Where is mom going to live when she comes out of rehab? And who is going to tell her that she can't go back to her condo? — which, I guarantee you from my experience in a nursing facility, is where she will want and expect to go.

Who is going to tell dad that he can't drive anymore? Will he listen to reason when his memory is going, or will you have to take away the keys? Sufferers of Alzheimer's can be very clever at masking their symptoms, especially if children do not see their parents often. My friend Kay only learned of her father's dementia when the police called her from a city ninety miles away to tell her that they had her father at the station and he did not remember where he lived.

Family dynamics come in to play when Mom does come "home." Your brother may say he can't take her because his wife won't have it. He may insist that it's Mom's own fault because she never treated her daughter-in-law that well. He says he'll "help with expenses." Little does he know how great those expenses can be.

Genworth, a financial and insurance company, published its "Cost of Care" Survey last year. Just to have a homemaker aide come in to help your aging parent keep the house clean runs $44,616 per year. If you need a home health aide, too, that's another $45,760 per year. Taking mom or dad to adult day care so you can go to work costs $17,904 yearly. An assisted living facility with one bedroom will cost $43,200 per year while a nursing home room, shared with one other patient, costs $80,300 per year. If you want mom or dad to have a private room in the nursing facility, the published cost is $91,250 yearly (Genworth, 2015).

Sometimes the only solution seems to be to take the aging parent into your own home. That is what Kay did when her father obviously could not be trusted to live on his own with access to a car. Kay worked second shift. After working the night before until 11 PM, she would rise early and fix her father's breakfast. She would then fix a lunch and a dinner to be stored in the refrigerator before leaving her dad in the care of her husband, who was retired. There was a constant worry on her part that her father would wander off or that he would fall. Even more concerning, she worried that her husband would grow tired of the minimal caretaking he was doing and refuse to do it anymore. Eventually, her father did regress until a nursing home was the only answer, with all the accompanying expense, pleas from the parent to "go home" and the unavoidable guilt.

If you think it will not happen to you, think again. Of the many millions in the baby boomer generation, more than 40% already contribute to their parents either in personal assistance or financially or both (Kennedy, 2010). Since people are living longer, we must assume that this is only the beginning. Just when you think you are finally free, you get to be the filling in the sandwich.

A financial maze exists for caregivers of older adults. Medicare pays for nursing home or home health care for only a short time. It pays for a rehab facility for three months. When that is gone, the caregiver must decide whether to give up working in order to devote themselves to elder care, for which they will not be paid, or whether to cobble together day care, household help and home health aides, all of which, as I have shown above, are expensive. Many care-giving children resort to legal help to get their aging parent on Medicaid after Medicare runs out and before every penny the elder parent has is gone to the expense of care (National Care Planning Council, 2011).

Teresa was left in this position. Her ninety-year-old mother had a condo on which dues had to be paid though she was expected to be in a nursing home for an extended time. Mom had about $5,000 in the bank. Teresa was obliged to use the services of an "elders" attorney, who charged her $2500, for advice on how to arrange these minimal assets in order to make Mom eligible for Medicaid. Having Medicaid pay for the nursing home after Medicare no longer applied preserved Mom's remaining funds to pay for small comforts in the nursing home and to pay the dues on the condo, thereby avoiding a lien on the condo when both Medicare benefits and her money ran out. Her children did not want a situation where their mother would have nowhere to go if the condo had to be sold for medical bills or was taken over by the homeowners' association for nonpayment of dues.

You may not approve of this maneuver. You may be thinking that Mom should have saved when she had the chance. Forget that idea. This is not a case of not saving. This is a case of living so long that the savings ran out. Financial assets which seemed perfectly adequate for retirement when Mom and Dad retired at 65 in 1990 are no longer adequate twenty-five years later. Dad died and his pension went with him. Due to inflation and the fact that ordinary savings do not pay the return they once paid, this mom and many like her are left nearly destitute.

Janey and Teresa and their fellow caregivers need all the help they can get. They try not to let their dependent child, grandchild or parent know what a strain they are under due to the extra duties. They don't want their loved ones to see themselves as a burden. Nevertheless, they ARE a burden and someone needs to help carry it! I have never understood why Medicare will pay a Home Health Aide, who has minimal training, to clean the house, to buy groceries, to bathe the patient or feed him, but Medicare will not pay a family member to do the same thing, even when the family member has had to give up a paying job to take on the care of a relative. The government is not only losing the taxes which the caregiver was formerly paying. The government is also paying far more for the Home Health Aide, who works for an agency, adding a middleman to the cost, than they would have to pay the family member directly.

There is a great deal of frustration involved in caring for parents who do not realize that they are not functioning as well as they perceive themselves to be functioning. As we have said, convention is one perpetrator in the rape of working women. Even when multiple children exist, it is still the daughter who gets the call when a family member becomes dependent. I experienced this myself when my father's mental acuity declined. I was the one to get the call when my stepmother complained to me about our father's increasing forgetfulness.

I took it upon myself to take Dad to the doctor and to monitor his prescriptions. I found that Dad was going to the VA clinic because his prescriptions were far less expensive there. However, he was seeing his regular doctor as well and filling more prescriptions for the same conditions, since he never told the doctor that he was being seen at the VA. No wonder his blood sugar and blood pressure were low. He was taking twice the medication he should have been taking. I worked it out with the help of his primary care physician for Dad to take the doctor's written recommendations to the nurse practitioner at the VA, whereupon, if she agreed, she would prescribe the recommended drug and Dad could get it at VA prices. This took several calls and checking up and I, of course, was working all the while.

Another problem was that, though I stressed what hours I worked and asked my father and stepmother repeatedly to make appointments during my off hours if they wanted me to attend, they repeatedly forgot and I found myself taking more time off to accompany them to morning or early afternoon appointments. As Dad got worse, I worried about whether he took the medications at all. He had a pill box with the days allotted but, since he often did not know what day it was, this was not helpful. I spoke to his doctor and arranged for a home health nurse to visit Dad, to arrange for his medication, to make sure he bathed and to check his vital signs.

If Medicare is to pay for such care, the consulting physician must have ordered the home health visit. I asked my father's doctor to do this and he complied. When the nurse got to the house, my father told her he didn't need her and would not let her in. He had completely forgotten that I had told him she was coming. The nurse apologized but said that, as long as he had not been judged incompetent, she was not allowed to enter the house without his consent. At this point, I was so distraught that I called my brother. My brother was the only one Dad listened to. Clay convinced Dad to let the nurse come in to help him the next time she visited, but I once again had to get the order and once again had to make the arrangements. It was infuriating to have Dad listen to Clay, who worked in the school system while I, who had worked in health care for many years, was ignored. I felt marginalized and insulted, though it was not my brother's fault. It was the fault of that bugaboo, tradition.

Caretakers of the elderly must be physically strong. This is not a toddler that you can pick up and carry. It takes strength to lift the wheelchair into the car, to help an infirm person into the shower or off the toilet. It also takes the patience of Job to wait while the elderly parent dithers about what purse to take or the location of his wallet. Then there is the effort of getting an infirm adult down stairs and into the car. If the caregiver is like me, work will be missed as well. According to *The Daughter Trap*, women lose 11.5 working years to care-giving responsibilities. Men lose only 1.3 years. Caregivers of the elderly will have to make time in their workday for phone calls either from the parent or for the benefit of that parent. Their concentration will be interrupted and, if things get unmanageable, the caregiver may have to take FMLA, that is, unpaid leave (Kennedy, 2010). If the situation does not get better and the caregiver must give up her job altogether, where does she get her own health insurance? There is the opportunity for COBRA for a period of eighteen months, but COBRA is very expensive since it includes the cost that is usually paid by the employer as well as by the employee.

All this and there's an emotional component. This mother or father that you are missing work to care for, to bathe, to feed, to take to doctors' appointments, may be the very parent who never gave you the love you needed, who destroyed your confidence with constant criticism, who did not provide financial support or who abused you. The truth is that you may not even like the person. Yet you will not only go on caring for them. You will deplete your own health and the family financial resources to do so. One source comes up with a figure of $5,531 per year for ordinary caregiver expense, close to 10% of the caregiver's income. That is money that the family would have had for their own use. If caregivers live a long distance from the parent, the amount is even more since they must hire outsiders to do more things (Kennedy, 2010). According to a study done by the Rosalynn Carter Institute, about a third of caregivers feel that their lives are richer because they have cared for a loved one. Another third muddle through; and the last third suffers a decline in health and premature aging (Sheehy, 2010). One has to wonder if this last third are those who are obliged to care for a parent who did not care for them.

Why do we take this on? For some, it is religious upbringing. We have been taught to put others first, to feed the hungry and to care for the sick. For some, it is true love. They feel that their parents deserve any amount of service. For others, perhaps most, it is duty. No one else is stepping up. I believe that it is these noble souls who suffer the most from the unremitting denial of self. These souls need help the most.

We have not spoken of the most common kind of care giving, the care we take of our immediate family; the cooking, the housework, the laundry, transportation of children, etc., etc. Things are changing but every survey I can find on how much time different members spend on household chores reports that the working wife/mother spends almost twice the amount of time on household chores as does the working husband/father. The jobs the husband/father does are the ones most often done on weekends; washing the car, mowing the lawn. Cooking is every night, laundry close to daily. Kid care is all the time. It is the endlessness of it that wears a woman down.

I do see the new generation of husbands/fathers picking up more of the chores, but not much has changed for my generation. For the men in my generation, their world has been turned upside down. Suddenly, in the 1960s or the 1970s, their wives went to work, probably because they needed the money or possibly just because they were bored to death. Suddenly, dinner was rushed, maybe late. She had the temerity to ask her husband or her son to vacuum, to clean toilets. Some acquiesced. Some rebelled. Most just went along, doing as little as possible and hoping somehow, someday, it would all go back to the way it was before.

When I retired, my husband and I came to an agreement on who would do what. He does the laundry and some cooking, which is very helpful, but I cannot depend on him to see the dirt on the floor and deal with it. He wasn't raised to deal with dirt or even to see it, and there have been women all his life who were only too happy to rush in and whisk the dirt away for him. Perhaps that is the biggest thing that has to change, the attitude of women. In her book, *Mom Incorporated; A Guide to Baby and Business*, the author quotes Julie Aigner-Clark, the creator of the popular Baby Einstein material. Ms. Clark states that it was very difficult for her to hire someone to do the things that she felt were her job (Smith D. E., 2011). Who told her that cooking and laundry were her job? We women say it to ourselves, and what gave us that idea? It is our nemesis, convention.

CHAPTER 11. HEALTH CARE COSTS TOO MUCH —
ESPECIALLY FOR US

The cost of health care is an issue with which I am familiar. My first supervisory job was in a small lab where I became intimately involved in billing. It wasn't supposed to be that way, but the girl who had been hired, before my employment, for the job of filing with Medicare turned out to be poorly trained and it became a group effort to fix all her mistakes. Prior to this experience, I was blissfully unaware of our three-price system for medical billing in the United States. We have the price for Medicare, the price negotiated by insurance companies and the price paid by the poor innocent who walks (or is carried) in off the street and is covered by neither.

Of course, the price of medical care affects all women, not just working women. However, if you are working then you are paying for your health care. Unless you are on a husband's plan, it is your paycheck that will get the deduction for health insurance and it is a big deduction. Insurance companies are in the business of making money. The reason your plan requires you to go to a certain lab, X-ray facility or hospital is that your insurance company has negotiated with that laboratory, radiation or hospital group to get discounted prices. David Belk, MD has posted a handy comparison study of common tests and procedures. His incentive for doing so is that he had a patient who thought she had a urinary tract infection, a UTI, but she had no insurance. Dr. Belk took it upon himself to find out the cost of a urinalysis for a person with no insurance. He was stunned to learn that the prices varied from $32 up to $92 for one of the simplest of laboratory tests. He found even the lowest price to be grossly inflated and this led him to discover the same startling fact that I learned when forced into the billing side of medical care. According to Dr. Belk's research, which is consistent with a recent Clinical Laboratory Diagnostic Fee Schedule, Medicare will pay the provider $4 for a urinalysis (UA) for you as a beneficiary. Private insurance has negotiated a price of $5 for the same test. However, the price in a hospital lab if you have no insurance is $92 for a simple urinalysis. This is not unusual. A Comprehensive Metabolic Profile, the kind we all get to check blood sugar, kidney and liver function, etc., costs Medicare $15, if they are covering the cost. Private insurance pays the same. If you walk in to a hospital lab with a prescription but no insurance card, you will pay $179 for the very same test.

Not only are lab tests priced differently; so are other procedures. For an EKG, one of the most common tests, both private insurance and Medicare will pay $26. The cost without insurance is $367! A chest X-ray that Medicare would cover at $41 and private insurance for $42, will cost the uninsured sufferer of chest congestion $375. Then there are the charges for a CT of the brain, commonly ordered to look for brain tumors; Medicare, $269.99, private insurance, $344 and uninsured, a whopping $2,621 (Belk, 2012-2016).

With surgical procedures, the difference in what various methods pay is even more surprising. Dr. Belk describes a patient with a hospital stay of two days duration. The total bill is $21,274.49. This included CT scans and an ER charge. The patient's private insurance, a Medicare Advantage plan, paid only $2,052.95, less than 10% of the total bill, and the patient was not liable for the remainder. He paid only a minimal co-pay. The hospital writes off the $19,000 and it writes off sums like that many times each day (Belk, 2012-2016). I have similar insurance and I see this kind of discount on my own bills. If this patient had not had an insurance company to negotiate his bill, he would have been on the hook for the entire $21,274.49. He might have been able to ask for an adjustment as charity, but you can bet that the discount would not be $19,000. Yes, Medicare Advantage is a sweet deal for us old folks and I am most grateful for it; but I am appalled at a system that allows such overcharging of other people. After all, if the hospital is making money, or at least getting by, on what Medicare and private insurance is paying, how can they ethically charge a person without these plans eight, or ten, or twenty times more for the same test or procedure? Yes, the government is backing Medicare and you, as a working person, are paying insurance premiums to the company to negotiate payments. The insurance company is risking that you will need less care than you are paying in premiums but, if the insurance company is paying only $2,052.95 on a bill Medicare approves at 21,274.49, it is obvious that the insurance company has some serious negotiating power. What is this power costing us taxpayers?

Not only is there an enormous disparity in amounts paid for tests and procedures, there is also a huge disparity in what hospitals bill for the same procedures. *The Tampa Bay Times* ran an expose of 50 US hospitals who charge the most for their services. The study focused on hospitals that charged more than 10 times the cost allowed by Medicare. The hospitals listed were found to be charging markups of from 920% up to 1,260% over actual costs. This means that a hospital visit that cost the hospital $300 in expenses could be billed at $3600 to an uninsured patient, to an out-of-network patient, and also to auto and workmen's compensation insurers. Seven of the 50 hospitals on the list are local to me. HCA, Hospital Corporation of America, runs five of the local hospitals. HCA is a for-profit corporation. Forty-nine of the 50 hospitals on the list are for-profit institutions. Representatives for HCA said that patients could apply for "charity care" or that they can ask for uninsured discounts which HCA purports are similar to the discounts a private insurance plan gets (Associated Press, 2015). Even if this is so, the problem is that patients don't know to ask for this discount. Instead, they are so blown away by the amount of the bill, they often make no effort to pay it at all and the hospital will ask the county, the state, or the Feds to kick in funds to cover indigent care. The money that will be coming from the county, the state or the Feds is your tax money.

I have heard people say that they believe for-profit health care to be superior since they "don't have to take the charity cases." For-profit hospitals cannot refuse an uninsured patient who shows up in the ER, nor would most health care professionals be willing to do so. The for-profit facility sometimes stabilizes that patient and ships him or her out to a not-for-profit facility, however; and it is true that non-paying cases are the source of a lot of red ink in the not-for-profit health care system. However, I have worked in ten hospitals over a long career, encompassing both not-for-profit and for profit hospitals. In my experience, not-for-profits are better staffed and better equipped than are the for-profits. For-profit hospitals have to pay their stockholders. Stockholders demand returns and, if the hospital chain can keep staffing to a minimum and avoid the cost of new equipment, that is one place to score the profit.

You can see that our medical system is complicated to say the least. Medicare has been a boon to doctors since it guarantees that they will be paid something but, given the cost of malpractice insurance and the amount of office help they need to handle the baffling insurance filing, a lot of doctors don't think Medicare pays enough. CNN gave examples of the amount paid to doctors for five procedures by both Medicare and private insurance, not Medicare Advantage plans. For an ordinary office visit, there is only a $6 difference between private insurance and Medicare reimbursement, but for low back surgery; Medicare would pay $654 while private insurance would pay the doctor $1,226 (Luhby, 2014). Some doctors in Florida, because of the large number of Medicare patients, are refusing to take new patients with Medicare as their primary insurer. Medicare has calculated how much doctors need to stay in business for each procedure for which Medicare pays. Perhaps the cost of running a medical practice has increased far beyond what it should cost to bill and get paid. Perhaps our system is so labor intensive that we need to make a change in how medicine is financed.

What are we getting for this money? According to the OECD, The Organization for Economic Co-operation and Development, which is a group of 34 member nations, the United

States spends 2 ½ times the average of the OECD members on health care. That is 17.6% of our Gross Domestic Product. Yet, the United States is at the bottom of the pile in terms of infant mortality, obesity and diabetes among all the wealthy member nations (Porter, 2016).

It would appear that we do not have the best medical care in the world, at least not all of us do, but we spend $8,233 per year per person on health care. Two reasons are given for the fact that our health care is so expensive. US doctors get higher incomes and they order more and more expensive tests. US doctors also operate under a fear of litigation (Kane, 2012). This is easy to understand since every other billboard on the highway is advertising a malpractice attorney. We also just discussed how doctors and hospitals get paid based on the procedures they actually do. It would seem that there is a powerful incentive to do more than might be necessary when a doctor is paid directly for the procedure. Medicare is trying to eliminate incentives that cause doctors to order drugs used in their own practice that are more expensive. As it is now, Medicare pays doctors the average sales price of a drug used inside the practice, such as a chemotherapy drug, plus a 6% bonus to cover administrative costs. One example is a drug for macular degeneration. For a drug that costs $2000 per treatment, that 6% is $120. Multiplied by dozens of patients, that adds up. There is a similar drug, quite possibly just as effective, that costs $50. Medicare is running a pilot program that pays doctors just 2.5% of the drug cost plus a flat fee to see if doctors will use less expensive but just as therapeutic options (Sanger-Katz, 2016).

Both France and Japan manage cost containment under their single payer system. They use a common fee schedule so that all doctors, hospitals and health services will be paid similar rates for most patients. In the US, some insurance pays more than others, with Medicare probably paying the least — so doctors can pick and choose among the best paying patients. A hospital stay in the US costs on average $18,000. In Canada, the Netherlands or Japan, the same stay would cost $4000 to $6000 less. The average stay among the OECD nations is $6,200 (Kane, 2012). Though health care costs less in these other countries, the quality of care is as good as or better than under our system and I have spoken to people from France, Germany, Australia, the UK and Canada to corroborate that fact.

One big difference in the cost of health care between countries is the cost of prescription drugs. As I stated earlier, the Veterans Administration long since negotiated with the pharmaceutical industry to get their patients drugs at a greatly reduced price. They were able to get this concession due to the volume of drugs that the VA doctors and nurse practitioners could be expected to order on such a large number of patients. Inexplicably, Medicare has never done that, though the number of patients insured under Medicare greatly exceeds the number insured under the VA. The VA is big, with 150 VA hospitals, 820 VA outpatient clinics and 8.92 million people enrolled in the VA health care system (Alba, 2014). However, Medicare is bigger with over 55 million enrolled beneficiaries (Kaiser Foundation, 2015), over six times the number in the VA, yet no discount has been obtained or even asked for. This is due to the enormously powerful lobby of the pharmaceutical companies in the United States. Having worked with Doctors without Borders in their clinic, I can attest to the differences between how drugs are ordered in the US and how they are ordered in other countries. Firstly, drugs are not called by their brand names in countries where medicine operates under a nationalized system. I had to get used to hearing the drugs used for TB or other conditions called by their generic names. Generics were the rule, not the alternative. I worked with Canadian and Australian doctors who told me they were not accustomed to drug reps visiting their offices on a regular basis and "updating" them on the newest and best brand name medicine. Since their government program was going to pay for an alternative new drug only if it had been proven more effective, they used the drugs that worked until they no longer did.

Nor do the pharmaceutical companies have the benefit of the human race in mind in their research. Only 10% of their research is done on the diseases that affect 90% of the world. Victoria Hale, who has secured grants from the Bill and Melinda Gates Foundation to work on drugs and strategies that combat diarrhea, malaria or other parasites says "At the executive level (of the pharmaceutical industry), it's almost all men. These executives decide which diseases to tackle, which products to develop." If it isn't likely to show a profit, that is, if it isn't likely to be useful in the wealthy Western world, it gets little, if any, funding. As an example, she talks about eclampsia, a life-threatening pregnancy complication. Drugs could be developed to combat the condition, but the lawyers for these executives advise against trying them on pregnant women due to liability issues. Hale formed OneWorld Health where drugs can be developed and trials run where the people live who need them (Dychtwald, 2010). I have seen pre-eclampsia in Africa. Had the woman I saw not had access to a Doctors without Borders clinic, and had we not transported her to a hospital where she could be delivered before full eclampsia developed, she would have died in misery. Believe me, that poor woman would not have been worrying about suing the drug company had there been a medicine available to save her. Women on the board of pharmaceutical companies could make a difference to all women.

I worked in small medical clinics for many years. Every Wednesday, the lab tech was kept late because the drug reps had taken up the doctors' time presenting new drugs, leaving samples and generally trying to convince the doctors that a new (and more expensive drug) would do a better job for the patient. Doctors were glad to get these samples as some patients could not afford to get prescriptions filled and the doctor could use these samples to get the patient started. They would never immediately decide to go to the newer drug but the suggestion that the drug might be an improvement had been implanted and doctors are very busy. Even the best don't always take the time to research each and every drug that comes on the market. It often takes some time before case studies come out that prove whether the old drug or the new drug is actually more effective or, quite possibly, that they work equally well. Then there are the doctors who benefit directly from ordering brand name drugs.

I've already mentioned that Medicare is trying to crack down on doctors who use more expensive drugs within their offices but there are other questionable practices. Analysts for ProPublica, an independent nonprofit newsroom, looked at doctors in five specialties who practiced in Florida and had 1,000 or more claims to Medicare in 2014. Of these doctors, 85% of them had received free meals or travel, gifts or compensation for speaking or consulting. The study found that the doctors who received the highest compensation were the doctors who prescribed the highest number of brand name drugs (McGrory, 2016). Florida has passed several laws to curb undue influence by drug or medical equipment companies but there are gray areas and there is no law against hiring a doctor to consult or speak and then paying them handsomely, creating good will. This good will costs the patient if they must pay extra for a brand name medication and it certainly costs Medicare if the doctor does not check the generic box.

Lest you feel sorry for the drug companies, who constantly tell us about the research they have had to do to bring new drugs to market, let me tell you that said research is often at least partially funded by the US government (National Academy of Sciences, 2009). Then the drug company makes the money back many times over, primarily from cost passed on to you, the American public. As an example, our dog had glaucoma. The vet prescribed Xalatan. My husband went to Walgreens to fill the prescription and was told that the cost would be over $100 for a 2.5 ml. bottle. That is a volume of one-half teaspoon. My husband then asked about a generic and was told that the cost would be $74.99 for the generic. We were aghast as our dog could be expected to use this drug three times a day for many years. We bought the first bottle at Walgreens but a Canadian friend suggested that we order the drug from Canada. We did so and got three bottles of the brand name drug, not the generic, for $61. That is 7.5 mls., three times the quantity, for over $200 less than in the US. We knew that the drug was the same because the pressure stayed down in the dog's eyes. That is only one example.

My dermatologist suggested that I use Retin-A, a strong preparation of Vitamin D, to clear my skin of pre-cancers that have developed from many years in the Florida sun. Retin-A is only approved for acne, so Medicare does not pay for it if used for other reasons. The cost for one 40-gram tube was an astonishing $338.95 at the cheapest local pharmacy. My sister had seen the same tube for sale in Mexico. We were in Arizona soon thereafter so we crossed into Mexico. *Pharmacias* were everywhere. I bought a large tube of brand name RetinA off the shelf, exactly the same, for $34. Obviously, other countries are not paying the same price for the same drugs that we are.

The drug companies are not satisfied, either, with overcharging us. One of the unfortunate impacts of the Trans Pacific Partnership agreement is purported to allow our pharmaceutical companies to extend their patents to countries that are now making affordable knockoff drugs for the developing world. Doctors without Borders, for one, depends on these lesser priced drugs. To allow our drug companies to force charitable organizations to buy drugs priced completely beyond their reach is to condemn many thousands to suffering and death. Our drug companies may do the research for the world but they are not entitled to hold the world hostage.

We are all paying for the government's failure to force drug companies to give Medicare a break in drug and required equipment prices. However, women are paying even higher prices for health care than is the general public. Supreme Court Justice Ruth Ginsberg stated, "Women of childbearing age spend 68% more in out-of-pocket health care costs than men" (Jacobson, 2014). This statement by Justice Ginsberg was in response to the decision by the Supreme Court that privately held corporations who objected to contraceptives could not be forced to pay for them as part of the health insurance offered to their employees. This ruling was in response to the mandate for coverage of contraceptives in the Affordable Care Act (Obamacare). This means that a woman who worked for a company run, say, by a Catholic organization, would not have the cost of her prescription for birth control pills covered by her insurance, but a woman working for a Protestant corporation would be able to fill her prescription under her insurance coverage.

Even including women over 65, the out-of-pocket expense for women in general was still 36% higher than men's. Just think of all those Pap smears, mammograms, bone densities and childbirth expenses. Men need none of those. As for contraceptives, the purchase of them is certainly benefitting the men in our lives, too. Yet, our court system is making it possible for our insurance to disallow them.

We know that women are taking the hit for all this extra medical expense when they pay out of pocket for something that their insurance should have covered. However, that is only a small portion of the disparity. You are again paying through the cost of your insurance coverage. Mercer LLC, an insurance and investment company, did a survey of Employer Sponsored Health Plans. They found that female employees pay an average of 13% more for their insurance coverage than do their male counterparts, considering premium contributions and deductibles. They used work forces made up primarily of female vs. male employees. Workers in predominantly female work forces paid $442 for a family PPO, while in predominantly male work forces, the cost was $338. Deductibles were also higher in the female work forces. An average in network deductible was $727 for the female workforce and only $557 for the male. Mercer makes the statement that "Not only are women being paid less, but their benefits go hand in hand" (Wojcik, 2014).

The Affordable Care Act (Obamacare) was supposed to make insurance equally priced for both men and women. This may be so, but it will take eternal vigilance to make sure it stays that way. It is true that some people have been able to get insurance through the exchange who did not have it before, but the Affordable Care Act is certainly not perfect. We still have the insurance companies setting the rates. Pre-existing conditions cannot exclude a buyer from coverage but there is no limit on what the insurance company may charge over time, possibly more than the insured can continue to pay.

As for everything else, the cost of health care weighs heaviest on the lowest paid workers. Under the Affordable Care Act, a woman making $29,000/year, though she qualifies for a premium tax credit, still pays over eight percent of her income in health care premiums. If she can only afford the cheaper plan, her deductible would be $2500. When the Affordable Care Act, went into force, the idea was for individuals with incomes below 138% of the federal poverty level, about $16,000 per year (2015 guidelines), to be covered by an expansion of Medicaid. The cost of the Medicaid expansion was to be covered almost exclusively by the federal government. However, some states, including Florida, refused this money (National Women's Law Center,

2014), leaving people with incomes at this level to try to buy coverage, which is not likely to happen. The small fine they will pay for not having coverage is much less than they would pay in premiums. Instead, they will do without insurance and show up in the Emergency Room of the nearest hospital, as they have increasingly been doing for decades. This will cost the taxpayers far more, when their state has to provide funds for indigent care, than would have been paid for the small portion of Medicaid not covered by the Feds. Of course, as we've already mentioned, the largest portion of indigent care is borne by not-for-profit hospitals and I believe it is no coincidence that the present governor of Florida is a former CEO of HCA, a for-profit hospital chain.

CHAPTER 12. WOMEN OVERPAY OVERALL

Have you ever heard of the Pink Tax? I had not but it is certainly to be discovered under multiple websites. The term was coined because female oriented merchandise sometimes costs more than that aimed at men, though the only difference between the two items is color, often pink. A study by the New York City Dept.. of Consumer Affairs found several examples of this tax. One was a girl's pink scooter, the same in every way except decoration. The girl's scooter costs $49.99 at Target while the boy's version sold for $24.99. According to the study, women's razors cost on average 11% more than men's razors. The difference is that women's razors are purple or pink. Overall, the study found that female consumers paid a mean 7% more for products similar to those marketed for men. Then there is the tampon tax. I was amazed to learn that in 40 out of 50 states, even those such as Florida that do not charge sales tax on drugs or food, tampons and sanitary napkins are taxed. California Assembly member Cristina Garcia has introduced a bill to exempt female sanitary products from sales tax. She says that only women must buy them so only women are being taxed. A similar proposal was made in Utah, which included exempting diapers from sales tax. Rep. Ken Ivory, part of a committee, voted no on the bill, claiming it would open the door to unlimited requests. FYI, it was an all-male committee. (Turner, Sam, 2016).

The researchers found big differences in toy prices beyond scooters. They mentioned the Raskullz shark helmet was priced at $14.99 while the Unicorn helmet aimed at girls was $27.99. That's a lot of money for a horn. Another was the Playmobil pirate ship at $24.99. The Fairy queen ship was priced at $37.99. The company declined to elaborate on price difference beyond possible production costs. How much more can a fairy cost as opposed to a pirate? Bad as toys may be, the largest price spread was in hair goods. Shampoos and conditioners meant for women cost a whopping 48% more than those supposedly for men. Clothing is another area where we pay more for the same thing. Among 24 retailers in New York City, there were clothing disparities of up to 24.6% between men's and women's similar garments. Levis showed the greatest variation in price. (Paquette, 2015). I can attest to the price gouging in clothing. I needed a simple nylon windbreaker and started looking in the women's department. All the jackets were in bright colors. I wanted the jacket for birding and bright colors are not recommended when looking for birds, so I wandered over to the men's department instead. Imagine my surprise when the men's windbreaker in black was priced at only $19.99 while the woman's jacket, the same except for color and a little trim on the pockets, was $29.99. The man's jacket was a little tighter in the hips but for $10 less for a flimsy piece of nylon, I decided I could live with it.

Incidentally, we pay these high prices despite the fact that the majority by far of our clothing is made in faraway lands where the people who make the fabric, cut the fabric and sew the clothes make very little. Last year Vera Bradley moved all of their manufacturing to China. The executives of Vera Bradley decline to say what the seamstresses make in China, though they firmly state that they "require that those wages meet the minimum wage requirements for the country in which they are working" (Huston, 2015). Vera Bradley reported net revenues of $154.1 million for the fourth quarter of their fiscal year, ending Jan. 2016, compared to $152.6 million in the prior fourth quarter (Vera Bradley, 2016) The stockholders won. American jobs lost.

Of course, American shoppers still pay the same $58–$109, for a Vera Bradley bag. I don't know of a comparable product made for men. Women are obviously targeted for these punishing markups. Benetton, a company that gets top dollar for their clothing, advertises that the garments are made in Europe. Technically, that may be so, but in Croatia garment workers supplying clothes for Benetton, though they may be paying what the county has deemed a minimum wage, actually make one third of what constitutes a living wage in that country's economy (Hoskins, 2014). Benetton also admitted in 2013 that some of the company's clothing was made in a factory in Bangladesh which collapsed, killing 900 workers (Evans, 2013). The CEO of Benetton was quoted as saying that he really believes companies such as his can improve the conditions for workers in countries such as Bangladesh (Evans, 2013). Yet, Human Rights Watch disclosed that two years after the disaster, factory managers were still not paying the country's minimum wage and were abusing any worker who tried to stand up for her rights. One union organizer in the factory was quoted as saying, "I was beaten with metal curtain rods in February when I was pregnant. I was called to the chairman's room and taken to the third floor management room which is used by the management and directors and there I was beaten by the local goons" (Human Rights Watch staff, 2015). Are the women in this country going to support this abuse of the women of the world? Maybe we American women should revolt against being gouged.

Not only do we pay more to buy our clothes, we also pay more to have them cleaned. CBS News sent two producers to several dry cleaners with cotton button down shirts. The shirts were the same except one was a man's shirt and one was a woman's. In half of the cleaners, the woman paid twice what the man paid and in one cleaner, the man's shirt cost $2.85 to clean and the woman had to pay $7.50 (Hatch, 2016).

Barbers usually charge both genders the same, but most hairdressers who specialize in cuts for women are more expensive than those who specialize in cuts for men. Some localities have rules that haircuts must cost the same regardless of gender, but that is a difficult rule to enforce when length of hair can be used as a reason to charge more. My hairdresser charges $35 for a cut with no styling. My husband gets his hair cut for $15.

One of the most likely places for women to get ripped off is at the car repair shop or the car dealer. In 1991, a professor from Yale Law School sent both men and women to car repair shops to get estimates on repairs. A white woman could expect to pay 40% more than a man for the same repair. A black woman would be charged an even higher fee (Paquette, 2015). The best defense against this, according to Essential Car Care for Women, is to educate yourself. "Go in sounding knowledgeable" says the author. Get recommendations from reliable friends and make sure you tell the mechanic to call you if he wants to do more work than was discussed (Little, Jamie and McCormick, Danielle, 2013). Researchers from Northwestern University found much the same thing. In 2012, they had call center agents call car repair shops in several cities. The agents asked about getting a radiator replaced on a certain car. The researchers knew that the repair should cost about $365. On average, female callers were quoted higher prices but, if the caller let the shop know that they were already aware of the approximate amount he or she should expect to pay, the price difference disappeared. If the caller intimated that she had done research, she was more likely to be given the proper price, $365. If the caller did not seem to have any idea what the repair should cost, the estimate went up as high as $510 (Kurtzleben, *US News and World Report*, 2013). It seems that it is buyer beware. Do your homework. Get more than one opinion about what is wrong with the car, then go to the Internet to find out what that repair should cost. Go back to the shop with some printouts.

When buying a car, there are good websites that will give you an estimate of what each kind of car will cost. I used Edmunds.com when I bought my car. They not only told me the approximate cost, they also rated the cars for endurance, gas mileage, etc. Still, being informed is not always enough. Women buy 54% of the cars purchased in the US but they dread going to look and with reason. Two economists did a study in Chicago using test subjects. Chicago car dealers quoted higher prices to female buyers even when the women were armed with the same prior information (Michon, 2016). Car salesmen can be pushy.

Remember that you don't have to buy immediately. If you aren't comfortable, go back and talk to a different salesman at another time. Take your prices from the internet if the price the salesman gives you is higher. Don't allow yourself to be patronized. You worked for that money. Make them work for theirs.

The same advice goes for home repairs. A woman in Virginia called a plumber for her overflowing toilet. He was in the yellow pages and she did ask in advance what the charge should be. She anticipated a bill of about $90 plus parts but was handed one for $929 (Holmes, 2015). In another instance, Jeff Rossen, a reporter for the Today show, used cameras in what was supposedly a woman's home to record different AC repairmen when they were called to fix a simple broken wire. The entire repair should not have cost more than $200. One AC tech wanted to charge the women an extra $200 for a part. Of course, the only part needed was a simple wire. One wanted to do work on an imaginary leak that would have run her an additional $492 and the last tried to charge this fictitious homeowner a staggering $950, which included a part that her particular AC unit did not even take (Powell, Robert and Rossen, Jeff, 2012). Closer to home, in my county, one enterprising contractor was investigated for shoddy home repair and home improvement. He charged female customers from $6500 to $23,900 for roof repair, painting and other fictitious labor. None of the work was adequate and he wasn't even licensed (Tisch, 2002). You may have noticed one commonality shared by all these victims. They were all women. Not that fraud is limited to women. My husband and I were almost victims of a dishonest AC repair person. Though we had used this company before, we were suspicious of his estimate. We asked our office manager for a list of companies that had been used successfully in this complex. Our doubts saved us about $4000. Get multiple bids. Get recommendations and, if it doesn't smell right, it is probably rotten.

A very expensive way in which to be taken advantage involves real estate. A 2011 study published by the *Journal of Real Estate Finance and Economics* found that women, on average, paid more for their mortgages than did men. Even when their credit scores were similar and other qualifications to borrow were the same, the women paid about 0.4% more for their mortgage. This amount becomes pertinent when you are going to be paying that mortgage for thirty years. In fact, when the woman pays a rate of 5.4% as opposed to the 5% a man may be paying, she may shell out an extra $26,000 over the life of the mortgage. The Authors of the study did not blame gender discrimination for the difference. Instead, they found that women were more likely to go to a certain lender because that lender was recommended to them. Again, women must do their homework, perhaps using an online tool such as LendingTree.com (Hill C., 2016). If you've done the research, have faith in your judgment. Trusting the wrong person can cost you money.

Women have enormous buying power. Reportedly, 83% of consumer purchases in the US are made by women and we can make ourselves heard. The market for organic milk is an example. I, like many others, decided to buy only organic milk after the doctor in our Molecular Department told us about the effect on growing girls of the additive, BCG. Bovine Recombinant Growth Hormone, given to dairy cows to increase the production of milk, has been suspected, though not proven, to be one reason for early puberty in girls. Our molecular doctor was not the only one convinced. The pediatrician of one of our techs told her to stop buying the milk from cows treated with this hormone. It may not be proven to cause early puberty here, but BHG is not allowed to be used in Europe or in Canada and mothers in the US didn't want to take chances. Suddenly, in 2008, the sale of organic milk rose to 22.5%, unheard of before BCG. Mothers had spoken (Dychtwald, 2010). We need to speak more often.

Women in business are also at risk of being overcharged. Christine Brenner became the new CEO of Brenner Metal Products Corp., a manufacturer of hospital beds. Suddenly, the suppliers of the raw materials needed to make the beds wanted about 20% more than the company had paid previously. Fortunately, Christine was able to ascertain from company records that she was being overcharged. The suppliers backed down as soon as they knew they had a well-informed woman at the helm. A like example is Kelley Evans, co-owner of a residential remodeling business. Kellie found out that her subcontractor was getting a better price than she and her partner were getting for the same product, a 33% better price. She did not use that supplier again. The experience made her aware that she had to check everything. Sure enough, she found her plumber was charging them double the amount he was charging the male contractors. Her reaction, other than to find a new plumber, was to join trade associations and make relationships with unbiased professionals who would give her straight answers (Fry, 2016).

We women are still up against the bimbo image. Some men love to take advantage of a woman because it bolsters their sick sense of superiority. The idea of being laughed at in the back room of the auto garage as well as wasting my hard earned money is enough to keep me on my toes. There are honest businessmen and businesswomen. We owe it to them and to ourselves to make sure they get our patronage.

CHAPTER 13. GOVERNMENT NEEDS US

We have discussed some of the reasons why women do not make as much as men and some of the ways they are obliged to spend more of what they make than men do. However, nothing affects your paycheck more than the government under which you live and work. The laws regarding minimum pay, overtime, FMLA, safety and health and taxes are all decided in government. Yet, who is running the government, or more specifically, your state and the USA? Today, women constitute 19.4% of the seats in the US House of Representatives and 20% of the US Senate. Women are governors in only six states (CAWP, 2016). Although there are 1800 women serving as state legislators, that is just 24.4% of the total number of 7400 state senators and representatives (NCSL staff, 2016). Since women actually outnumber men in this country, 51% to 49% approximate (Henry Kaiser Family Foundation, 2014), we should certainly be represented to a great extent. So, why aren't we and what would happen if we achieved that equality in government?

A survey by Political Parity asked questions regarding the reason why women do not run or, if elected, do not run for higher office. The responders said that fund raising requirements and party support were the biggest barriers to running for election. About half felt that their political party supported men and women equally and the other half believed that men got more encouragement. No one felt that women were encouraged above men. As for fund raising, one reason was their lack of "networking." The women did not find an easy inroad to the network of movers and shakers that support, donate and spread the word on a candidate (McGregor, *The Washington Post*, 2014).

I remember very well a nugget of wisdom imparted to me by a pathologist with whom I worked many years ago. We were speaking of the candidates in a local election and I bemoaned the fact that none of them were of high caliber. I said, "There have to be better qualified people." Dr. Winter said to me, "Jo, you and I are thinking people. We don't run for office because we feel we don't know enough about the job the office entails. We feel that we might not be qualified. The people who are running are too dumb to know their limitations."

Is this what we have come to in our elections? Are the candidates the ones who have the networking, who have the support of the Super Pacs but are themselves too dumb to know their limitations? Some who have run are clearly not the best and brightest so perhaps they don't worry about whether they are qualified. They're just after the money and the perks. The pay certainly isn't bad. A beginning US Senator or Representative makes $174,000 per year. Of course, a Minority or Majority Leader makes more, $193,400 per year, and the base salary for the Speaker of the House is $223,500. The perks are significant. Both Social Security and the Federal Employees Retirement System cover members of Congress. They have great health care coverage and receive a Representational Allowance of $944,671 to use for hiring staff plus additional allowance for office expense and mail (Brudnick, 2014). Of course, Congress isn't always in session so many still retain private businesses or careers while they serve.

It sounds like a sweet deal. A mother in Congress can take her children with her to Washington or she could go home on weekends, so what's the problem? The Hampton Institute, which bills itself as a working class think tank, says that Congress "resembles a frat house where young intoxicated men are replaced with middle aged men, and the type of policies voted upon, discussed and proposed ... reflect the group think that occurs with members of a fraternity" (Charleswell, 2015). We aren't being admitted to the fraternity, ladies. By virtue of our sex, the good old boys deem us unacceptable and it is the good old boys who are buddies with the fundraisers. I believe that if real campaign reform could be implemented today, we would see a lot more female candidates.

The reason it is important for working women to be aware of women in politics is because it has so often been women in government who have been responsible, in large measure, for the legislation that has helped us; FMLA, civil rights, Title IX, child-care, The Pregnancy Act, etc. Yet in 1998 the US ranked fifty-ninth in the world for percentage of women in its national leg-islature. By 2014, we were ninety-eighth. That put us just ahead of the United Arab Emirates. Cynthia Terrell of FairVotes "Rep-resentation 2020 project" says that, at the current rate of prog-ress, "Women won't achieve fair representation for nearly 500 years." This situation continues despite various studies, which have shown that having women in office makes a significant dif-ference in the kind of laws that are passed.

Former Political Science Association president Arend Lijphart found that women were associated with more laws regarding the environment, support for families and bills that dealt with prison reform and prevention. Health and education would have had few champions had it not been for female legis-lators. (Hill S., 2014). Let's look at what female legislators, still in office today, have accomplished:

- Sen. Mazie Hirono, a Democrat from Hawaii, has consis-tently been a champion of women's rights, the rights of the elderly and veterans.

- Sen. Debbie Stabenow, a Democrat from Michigan, was a co-sponsor of the Lily Ledbetter Act. Sen. Stabenow is a mother and grandmother.

- Sen. Elizabeth Warren (Democrat, Massachusetts) was a Harvard law professor; a mother of two, she has been active in financial reform after the Wall Street melt down.

- Sen. Maria Cantwell (Democrat, Washington) is a fighter for the environment and for alternative energy.

- Sen. Patty Murray (Democrat, Washington) was a preschool teacher with two children of her own. She chairs the committee on veteran's affairs.

- Sen. Diane Feinstein, a Democrat from California and a mother, is Chair of the Committee on Intelligence, the first women to hold that position. She has raised at least $65 million for breast cancer research.

- Sen. Barbara Boxer, a mother and a Democrat from California, is a defender of reproductive rights for women and has co-sponsored bills to improve women's access to health care. Rep. Boxer has announced that she will be retiring at the end of her term.

- Sen. Heidi Heitkamp (Democrat, North Dakota) is a breast cancer survivor and environmental lawyer. She brings common sense to the healthcare law.

- Sen. Amy Klobuchar, also a mom, and a Democrat from Minnesota, was named by *Working Mother Magazine* as "best in Congress" in 2008.

- Sen. Susan Collins, Republican from Maine, has never missed a roll call vote in the Senate and is well respected by members of both parties.

- Sen. Barbara Mikulski is the Senate's longest serving female senator. She has been in office over twenty-five years. She says that she was a social worker, serving Baltimore families and now (serving in the Senate) she is a social worker building opportunities for families throughout America. Sen. Mikulski believes that "When women are in the halls of power, our national debate reflects the needs and dreams of American Families." She was instrumental in setting the standards for mammograms and for legislation that prevents elders from going bankrupt when they have to pay for a spouse's nursing home care.

- Sen. Jeanne Shaheen, mother of three and grandmother of seven, is a Democrat from New Hampshire. Sen. Shaheen has been a player in the fight to lower the cost of prescription drugs and to make generics more available. She has been an indefatigable defender of women's rights.

- Sen. Kirsten Gillibrand, Democrat from New York, has two young sons and has used her office to further progress on childcare and education.

- Sen. Kelly Ayotte, Republican from New Hampshire, has opposing views on some issues but she is in favor of limiting medical malpractice claims, a move that many believe is necessary if the cost of medical care is ever to be controlled. She opposes entitlement programs as they now exist and our country has always depended on different views in order to reach balanced decisions (Keller, 2012).

Member of the US House of Representatives have also made notable contributions to the betterment of women. The first woman to be elected to the House was Jeanette Rankin, elected in 1916, four years before women officially had the right to vote!

Women in state legislatures have also made a difference. In 1912, Ruth Hanna was elected to the Illinois legislature. She was a mother of three and had already proven herself to be a mover and a shaker when, finding unsanitary conditions on Illinois dairy farms, she opened a dairy and breeding farm in Illinois for the purpose of providing clean milk for invalids and children. Mrs. Hanna maintained a pro-suffrage agenda during her tenure in the Illinois House, then went on to be elected to the US House of Representatives in 1928 as a Republican. She organized women's groups within her party and was deeply concerned for the lives of women and children (US House Office of the Historian, 2007).

There was no law in South Carolina against stalking until women began serving in their government. The men never thought to pass any laws like that. The joke among the women was, "Yeah, because nobody stalks old fat guys" (Dychtwald, 2010).

Though it is not well known, the Equal Rights Amendment was actually proposed in 1923, the culmination of work by Susan B. Anthony and Sojourner Truth, who had tried to have the rights of women, including the right to vote, included in the fifteenth amendment, which gave the vote to men of color. However, women were left out of that amendment and had to wait another fifty years to have the same right to cast a ballot (Francis, 1998).

After women were finally allowed to vote in 1920, the Equal Rights Amendment was rewritten by Alice Paul in 1943 to read: "Equality of rights under the law shall not be denied or abridged by the United States or by any state on account of sex." This amendment attempted to address other inequalities as to pay and equal treatment. In its new form, it came up for a vote again, twenty years after its inception. Claire Booth Luce, another Republican mother, was one of the most visible female members of the US House of Representatives. Rep. Luce is known for her involvement in the United Nations Relief Agency after World War II. She supported the Equal Rights Amendment when it came up again and, when that failed to pass, she introduced a bill in 1946 to assure that women and minorities got equal pay for equal work (US House Office of the Historian, 2007).

Motherhood was already an issue when Emily Douglas was elected to the US House of Representatives in 1944 while she was the mother of an eleven-year-old daughter. Rep. Douglas admitted that being a mother as well as a member of Congress posed a challenge since the wife of a male representative might be "happy and proud to pull up stakes, corral her children and move to the designated center of government," while a woman in that position had to consider her husband's business and her children's school. Yet she contended that being a mother with familial duties gave her a "unique perspective on legislation." She knew she had a personal knowledge of the price of groceries and other necessities that male members might not have. She said the "kids were her motivation." They became, she said, "my reason for striving" (US House Office of the Historian, 2007).

Chase Going Woodhouse served in two separate terms as a Representative from Connecticut beginning in 1945. Rep. Woodhouse was influenced by her grandmother who took her to polling places as a child, where her grandmother would protest against being excluded as a woman from voting. In the 1930s, Woodhouse founded the Institute of Women's Professional Relations to study the status of working women while she was working and raising two children herself. She held advanced degrees in economics and was instrumental in establishing the International Monetary Fund and the World Bank. She felt strongly that the strong economic co-operation between nations would help not only to win the war but would help with the rebuilding afterwards. Woodhouse also advocated for rural electrification and more money for education (History Art and Archives staff, na).

During the 1970s, female members of the House advanced the causes of women. Bella Abzug, a mother of two, ran for office with the slogan that "A woman's place is in the House-the House of Representatives." Ms. Abzug had applied to Harvard Law School in the 40s but was denied entrance because of her gender. The refusal only encouraged her zeal for reform and, after graduating with a law degree from Columbia, she distinguished herself with her legal defense of a black man in Mississippi, accused of raping a white woman, and also her defense of victims of the Joseph McCarthy witch hunt. Rep. Abzug fought for civil rights as well as for the rights of women (Biography.com).

Patricia Schroeder was elected to the House in 1972. She made no secret of having a six-year-old and a two-year-old, and made juggling career and family a way of life. She kept diapers in her bag at the House and crayons in her office. She made the statement that, "being a working mother, whether you're a Congresswomen or a stenographer, means that everybody feels perfectly free to come and tell you what they think, 'I think what you are doing to your children is terrible.' 'I think you should be home.' They don't do that to men." Though she maintained that she could handle the pressure, even she had doubts, admitting that shortly before she began the job, she thought to herself, "What's a mother like me doing here? I'm about to be sworn into Congress and I haven't even potty trained my daughter." Yet, Rep. Schroeder went on to expand Social Security benefits and to focus on women's health care and child rearing and was a supporter of the Equal Rights Amendment. She was one of those instrumental in the passing of the 1978 Pregnancy Discrimination Act, which said that employers could not dismiss female employees just because they were pregnant or deny them health and disability benefits. Perhaps her crowning achievement was the passing of the Family and Medical Leave Act, which we have talked about before, the only resort Americans have to keeping their jobs in the face of a family health issue (US House Office of the Historian, 2007).

We can't leave out Nancy Pelosi, mother of five, who came from a political family but got into politics slowly, beginning with volunteering for the Democratic Party. She was elected to the US House of Representatives in 1987. She has been a tireless advocate for health and housing initiatives and for human rights in general. Pelosi has earned a place in history as being the first female Democratic Leader of the House of Representatives and the first female Speaker of the House. She is now the Minority Leader of the House (Biography.com).

These are just a few of the women who serve or have served in Congress, but you can see that, in general, they serve women well. Of course, there have been female senators and representatives that only served themselves and it is never wise to vote for a candidate just because she is a woman but if both candidates are equally qualified, I tend to support my sister.

New candidates are getting into the political arena. Rep. Gwen Graham, a Democrat and the daughter of former Florida Governor Bob Graham, is considering running for governor of Florida in 2018 (Klas, 2016). Gwen Graham was born into politics, as her father was not only governor of Florida but also a US Senator and briefly a contender for the presidency. Bob Graham was one of our best governors and I am still angry with the press for making fun of him while he was running for the Presidential nomination. They seemed to find it amusing that he wrote items down in his little notebook for further review. To me, that meant he actually intended to address the issue at hand instead of glibly tossing off a vague promise and promptly forgetting about it. I have read Gwen's bio and she appears to be a chip off the old block, tackling serious problems such as the pollution of our springs here in Florida and the slowness of getting veteran's benefits. Indeed, her father's office finally got my father the health benefit he had been due since World War II. Gwen has worked side by side with Florida workers to learn how it is in the real world. She worked briefly on farms, as a hotel maid and even in a jet on an Air Force base. She is 53 and has three children. This is the kind of representation American working women need (Gwen Graham staff, 2016).

There have been, and still are, women in the Legislature, who do not agree with the Equal Rights Amendment, with funding Planned Parenthood or with some programs helping the disadvantaged. Michele Bachmann and Sarah Palin come to mind. Both have five children and should be able to speak to the problems of working mothers. I don't see that their agendas have furthered that cause but they have a right to run, to voice their opinions and their constituents have a right to vote for them. That's the American way. We simply have to field more female candidates with varying views so that there is real choice. That might entail a different kind of electoral system.

The old guard does not seem to be in danger of falling any time soon but there is growing dissatisfaction with the two-party stranglehold. The number of members each state can send to the US House of Representatives depends on the population of that state. However, in order to keep the number of Representatives to a manageable level, able to fit into the House building, the total number was capped at 435 in 1911, with five more non-voting members from our Territories.

Our present federal system is a winner-take-all operation with each congressional district electing the one candidate who gets the majority of votes in that district even if the ratio is 49:51. The US Constitution does not require the use of single seat districts; that is, there could be more than one party represented from a single district if that state is allowed to elect more than one representative. One possibility is the multi-seat district where political parties win seats in proportion to the percentage of the votes they received. This is also called Proportional Representation. Under a multi-seat district system, in a state that is allowed ten representatives, if a political party got 10% of the vote, that candidate would get one seat in the US House. If the party got 50% of the vote, that party could send five representatives. We would have a much more varied House of Representatives that would far better represent the will of the people they serve.

One example of a multi-seat system would be Germany's arrangement where the Green Party won only 11% of the total vote but still is represented in their governing body. The Green Party also has a 50:50 rule for candidates requiring an equal number of men and women on the ballot. New Zealand also uses a multi-seat system and has more women in government than does the US, particularly at the local level (Hill, S., 2014).

Some states already use a multi-seat system in at least one of their legislatures. Women win more seats in this kind of system. The Vermont State Legislature has 41% women, elected under a multi-seat system. Arizona also has this kind of system and they have 36% women. The average percentage of female state legislators in single-seat systems is 23% (Representation 2020, na).

It was not until 1967 that Congress passed a law requiring one representative per Congressional district. That law could be changed to allow a Proportional Representation system. It might be a solution to the deadlock we see in our politics today, with each side fairly evenly matched, dug in to their own agendas and not budging one inch to get anything done for the country.

Changing to a multi-seat system is only one suggestion toward election reform. Everyone I know believes that we have to get the Political Action Committees (PACs) out of politics. Money is running the show and it is money that could be better spent. If candidates were not allowed to accept contributions from big business, they would not arrive in their new offices already indebted to their donors. A bill has been introduced that could bring about election reform. It is called the Fair Elections Now Act, introduced by Congressman John Yamuth along with 52 co-sponsors. Eight of the co-sponsors are women, several of whom were mentioned above. This bill would require a candidate for the House of Representatives to raise a large number of small contributions limited to $100 each. The minimum amount he or she would have to raise is $50,000, all of it from people in his or her state. This requirement not only helps to fund the election, it also proves that the candidate is serious and has broad support. For a Senate race, the bill suggests a base of 2,000 donations plus 500 donations for each of the state's districts. That is: as Florida has twenty-seven districts, a person running for the Senate from Florida would need 2,000 donations plus a further number of 27 x 500 or a total of 15,500 donations to be placed on the ballot. No donation could be for more than $100 for one year.

If candidates raised the required amount of support, they would receive Fair Elections funding. House candidates would get a total of $1,125,000, 40% for the primary and, if he or she won, the rest would be for the general election. For the Senate, a qualifying candidate would get $1,250,000 plus another $150,000 per congressional district in his or her state. The split would be the same, 40% for the primary and 60% for the general election. Candidates could continue to receive small contributions from people in their home states and get matching funds but there would be a limit of how much money could be spent.

I'm sure you are asking, as I did, where this money is coming from. Most taxpayers would not want to fund multiple elections. The money will come from a small percentage levied on the largest recipients of government contracts. There would be no loyalty owed to any contractor because no specific candidate would benefit. It's a clever idea and the contractors can afford it. The Dept.. of Defense awards contracts of Seven Million Dollars or more every weekday at 5 PM (US Dept. of Defense, 2016). In 2014, the last year for which the data is available, Lockheed got almost $32 billion in government contracts. Boeing got $19 billion. The total amount awarded in government contractors in 2014 was $439 billion (Aeroweb staff, 2015). These contractors are very well paid. It has been reported in numerous sources that government contractors make up to three times more than do private sector wages. Furthermore, spending on those government contracts has increased by 45% during the last ten years (Porter L., 2014). It sounds like they could afford to give a little back by way of some general campaign financing rather than giving it to the specific candidate that they know will reward them with even more lucrative contracts.

Another suggestion for more just elections is Instant Runoff Voting. This idea would eliminate the fear we all have that, by voting for an independent candidate, we will be handing the election to the candidate we want least. In Instant Runoff Voting, voters rate the candidates in order of preference. That is, if you wanted to vote for an independent, you would rate that person as your first choice. You might rate the Democratic candidate as your second and the Republican candidate as third. If your first choice did not get enough votes to wine, your vote would go to your second choice. This system eliminates runoff elections, which are expensive (Jilani, 2010).

Lastly, we could make voting day a holiday and allow people to register and vote on the same day (Jilani, 2010). Wouldn't that make it easier for working women and men? Our present system is outdated. It does not take advantage of computer technology to check voter eligibility or to give us real choice instead of having to choose the lesser of two evils between increasingly negative warring parties.

Not only would campaign reform make us more fairly represented in government, it could make a lot of money available for rebuilding our crumbling infrastructure. As of April 2016, the candidates in the US Presidential election alone have raised $1,221,000,000. That money will go strictly for the purpose of getting elected (*The New York Times*, 2016). The vast bulk of this money came from just 158 individuals and families including those dealing in oil, hedge funds, entertainment and other ventures (Confessore, Nicholas; Cohen, Sarah; Yourish, Karen, 2016). Just think, if that money could have been paid into US taxes, $1,221,000,000 would fix some bridges, update some power grids or put more money into education and child care. That money could replace some of the money that is being taken out of your paycheck. A side benefit would be that we, the American public, would not be deluged by campaign ads and mudslinging news flashes for a solid year before the election is even held.

The men of this country have had two hundred and fifty years to make changes. It is time for women to see what we can do. I don't think the answer is to play more golf and drink more martinis so as to fit into the present networking structure. The lack of diversity in corporate boardrooms and in political parties has resulted in the stagnation we see now. Witness the Detroit auto industry. Some of those companies relied on hiring their cronies, the people they knew to be like them, to staff their Boards. No new blood, no new ideas, and they lost an enormous part of the market share to Japanese imports that satisfied the needs of the American people. More women in their boardrooms might have foreseen those needs. We need to reform that power structure. We need to network with other people who see the bigger picture and who want to see progress. The League of Women Voters does not campaign for any particular candidate but they do help to get people registered and involved. They provide a support group for women who believe that we could change government if more of us were in it. We must be convinced of our own abilities and be able to convince the insiders of our abilities, too.

A step in that direction is coming from Emerge America. This group both encourages female candidates to run for office and trains them to win when they do. Emerge America has a seven-month, 70-hour training program for Democratic candidates. They have 315 of their alumnae running for office in 2016 (Emerge America staff, 2016). Who among you will take the course?

Chapter 14. Stress Exacts Payment

I'm sure that I don't need to tell you about stress. Any woman who is holding down a job, raising kids, keeping a house and possibly trying to keep a marriage thriving is already quite familiar with stress. Some surveys reported by the American Institute of Stress attribute 75–90% of visits to primary care physicians to stress related ailments. Just a few of the physical manifestations are: eating disorders, stomach ailments, skin reactions, depression, sleep problems, heart disease and autoimmune responses (Kittredge, 2015).

Even so, you may wonder why I am including a chapter on stress in a book focused on how you are victimized financially. I include it because stress will cost you money, for health care and as a result of the self-medication many of us use to cope with stress.

Research has shown that women are 2–3 times more likely than men to have depression or anxiety disorders, both often the results of stress. Whether we like it or not, we are all the instruments of our brain. It is the master controller and the chemicals, which the brain triggers, flow into our bloodstreams, affecting the way we feel and behave.

For instance, you are at work and you can't find an important paper that the boss is requesting. People are waiting and you feel flustered. First, the brain reacts to stress stress by secreting substances to gear up the adrenal glands. Adrenaline, from the medulla of the adrenal glands, makes us ready for fight or flight, upping our blood pressure and heart rate, triggering the release of blood sugar to the cells to give us extra energy. Adrenocorticotropic Hormone, ACTH, comes from the pituitary and stimulates the release of cortisol. Cortisol, from the outer part or cortex of the adrenal gland, is released in order to sustain this hyperactive state of the body. If the paper you are looking for is located, or the boss is able to get along without it, the amount of stress hormones will level off and your blood pressure will start to come down. However, if instead it becomes a treasure hunt with the whole office searching for one paper, which was your responsibility, those stress levels stay high. Blood sugar is consumed by the galvanized response, fatigue sets in and you go home exhausted whether the paper was ever found or not. Human beings were never meant to stay in revved up mode for long periods. High levels of cortisol are not usually detectable in the blood in ordinary stress disorders but, if you are under unrelieved stress, you can bet that your adrenal cortex is putting out intermittent bursts of cortisol trying to keep your body up to meeting the demand. It is when this demand goes on and on that we suffer the negative effects of stress. Continuing high levels of cortisol can suppress the immune system.

High levels of cortisol have been implicated in cognitive dysfunction in older people including decline in language skills, processing speed, eye-hand co-ordination and verbal and visual memory (Lee BK; Glass, TA; McAfee MJ; et al., 2007). Could it be that the non-stop stress of our everyday lives may be contributing to the likelihood of developing Alzheimer's in later life? Scary!

So far, both sexes are subject to the same reactions. Then the sex hormones kick in. Men are subject to their own sex hormones, of course, but women's sex hormone levels fluctuate too, and this makes our biology much more complicated. From puberty to menopause and even beyond, our hormones affect us. Estrogen, testosterone, progesterone and the thyroid hormones all contribute to our sense of wellbeing or lack thereof and, while the levels are fluctuating monthly, our moods can fluctuate, too.

There are other neurotransmitters, substances that allow transmission of impulses from one area of the brain to another that influence our thoughts and actions. Serotonin is one of them and serotonin has been shown to be a powerful force for good or evil. Many areas of the brain are affected by serotonin, including those associated with mood, sexual desire, appetite, memory and sleep. Most of us know that low levels of serotonin have been associated with depression, but lack of this vital chemical can also lead to obsessive-compulsive disorder, anxiety and panic disorders. Some studies have shown that the female hormones interact with serotonin leading to the mood shifts many of us suffer during menstrual periods or childbirth. Men produce half again as much serotonin as women (Nishizawa, Benkelfat,Young,, et al., 1997). This physiological difference may explain why women are more likely than men to report being stressed and to report that the stress is worsening.

Some of our stress is brought about by our own perception of responsibility. How often have you looked at the mildew in the shower, the dusty baseboards, the dirt around the doorknobs and felt stressed because you don't know how you will ever get to it or even where you will get the energy to start? Your job and making meals and riding herd on the kids sucks up all of your energy on a daily basis. Yet the mildew bugs you. It also bugs you that the time you spend with your kids is taken up with yelling and prodding, not what you would call quality time, while your husband manages to live in another world, staring at a ballgame or entranced by the computer, oblivious to the mildew and the dirt. This is stress and it takes many names: guilt, depression, anxiety, resentment, fatigue, apathy (Kennedy, 2010).

Women are more likely than men to feel stress about money. One might attribute this to the fact that women make less money and would likely find it harder to support a family, but The American Psychological Association found that married women are more likely to think money or the lack of money is a cause for stress. Married women report higher levels of stress than single women do. One reason would seem to be that they not only have a job and kids to worry about. They stress about their husbands, too. About half of women, in general, report that they react to stress by eating either too much or unhealthy foods. They say they are too tired to summon up the willpower to change. It will probably come as no surprise to you that six times as many women as men feel that having more help with household chores would help with their will power (American Psychological Assoc., 2016).

I always associated stress with depression. Seeing no end to the chores both at work and at home is enough to make anyone depressed, especially as we grow older and our energy wanes. The National Institute of Mental Health published a handy, dandy booklet on women and depression. It lists the symptoms of depression as:

- Feeling sad or empty
- Feeling hopeless irritable anxious or guilty
- Loss of interest in favorite activities
- Feeling very tired
- Not being able to concentrate or to remember details
- Not being able to sleep or sleeping too much
- Overeating or not wanting to eat at all
- Thoughts of suicide or suicide attempts
- Aches and pains, headaches, cramps or digestive problems.

The website gives advice to friends or loved ones of the depressed woman. It advises taking her out for walks, talking to her and offering her moral support (National Institute for Mental Health, 2016). All this is good, but not once does the Institute for Mental Health recommend going over to her house and; doing the laundry, taking meals in so she doesn't have to cook or better yet, taking her out to eat, cleaning the shower or taking the kids off her hands for a day. There is no specific author for this article but I doubt it was written by a wigged out working mother.

It is said that women are genetically predisposed to stress and are twice as likely to suffer major depression as men. As stated, we have our hormones to contend with and we do tend to obsess more about our relationships, trying to "fix" everything and everyone we care about. Seasonal Affective disorder is four times more common in women, suggesting a difference in the female brain that makes the loss of light particularly trying. But

The National Institute of Science acknowledges that a big factor is that married women and (former) housewives have entered the workforce and "find it difficult to juggle job and family responsibilities, such as caring for an elderly relative" (Chairman's Blog, 2014). Society has continued to see us as the caregivers while men have largely been allowed to remain the cared for. Children, too, can eat away at their mother's reserves with their incessant cravings. Instead, they should take on responsibility in the household. A school age child can set the table, carry the plates to the kitchen and even learn to load the dishwasher. They are eager to show how "big" they are at that age. Do them a favor and bring them up the way you think the family of the future should be.

The flip side of depression is anxiety. It is perfectly possible to suffer from both at different times. Nearly two-thirds of the 57 million adults who are diagnosed with anxiety disorder are women. Anxiety is described as unwarranted fear or distress. Women are anxious about their health or that of their family, about having enough money and some are afraid of being compared to others and found wanting (Harvard Medical School staff, 2008). All of these are normal worries but with anxiety, the fears cannot be allayed, even when things are going well. The anxiety comes from stress. While some women feel tired and depressed looking at the moldy shower, others feel anxious and will drive themselves to exhaustion trying to keep up with everything. Anxiety has been linked to heart disease. In the Nurses' Health Study women with a high level of nervous anxiety were 59% more likely to have a heart attack than less affected women. They are prone to panic attacks and obsessive-compulsive disorder. Perhaps the most common symptom is gastrointestinal: an upset stomach and or abdominal pain and bloating, even vomiting and diarrhea. It isn't hard to understand why anxiety could lead to health problems. The body is in high gear all the time. While a certain amount of stress is natural when facing a big test or presentation, the body needs down time, too.

A *Glamour* reader described the pressure she feels in her life. She has begun to have panic attacks and blames it on her "to do list." She is trying to excel in a stressful job, then go home and cook dinner (a perfect one, no doubt), work out (to keep that perfect figure), check in with friends and family, and still have time and energy for her boyfriend. This reader is suffering from panic disorder, a not uncommon condition. The attack is described as heart pounding, dizziness and a feeling of dread. There are two other kinds of anxiety disorders. One is a sort of phobia in social situations. I think most of us are a little unnerved when we enter a room where we are expected to mix and we know no one, but in a person with social anxiety, that situation may bring on a stress headache, an upset tummy or worse. Lastly, there is a generalized anxiety, which manifests as nagging worry (Dreisbach, 2010). The mind tries to put a label on this worry and winds up being worried about everything.

My friend Kay experienced panic attacks. She was the tech who was working full-time while she also had her father at home with worsening Alzheimer's and a husband who didn't like the situation. Sometimes her brain overloaded on stress hormone and she would wind up in the ER. There was usually a period of calm after that, as her husband was temporarily convinced that she was doing too much and she got a period of enforced rest. It is a bitter reflection on a society that this is what it takes for a caretaker to be cared for.

There is even a new kid on the block found to be a factor in panic attacks, a hormone by the name of orexin or hypocretin. Levels of orexin, discovered in 1998, are known to be low in people suffering from narcolepsy, a disorder marked by periods of inadvertent sleep. Conversely, levels of orexin in the cerebrospinal fluid of patients suffering from panic attacks have proved to be elevated. Panic attacks can be induced in rats by infusing an ordinary salt of sodium lactate which causes the release of orexin the brain. Moreover, when researchers blocked the gene in rats which coded for orexin, the same rats no longer demonstrated the panic symptoms (National Institute of Mental Health, 2009). A study published in the *Pharmacological Review* revealed that orexin, secreted by the hypothalamus of the brain acts to stimulates the adrenals and to bring about the release of our old friends adrenaline and cortisol (Spinnazi, R; Andreiz, P.; Rossi, G. et al., 2006).

Our cell phones and computers add stress, as well, since we are always "in touch" and calls, texts and e-mails vie for attention. The pharmaceutical industry would like us to believe that they have come to our rescue with uppers and downers and there is certainly a place for medication but it is too often just covering up the problem. Women are more stressed than men because more is expected of us.

We are probably all guilty of wolfing down a Snickers bar and a cup of coffee about 4 PM when our blood sugar level is low and we are trying to get the day's work finished. There is a reason why women eat the wrong things and overeat when stressed. Harvard studies have shown that when animals undergo chronic and prolonged stress, cortisol increases appetite and can lead to obesity. Stress also caused animals to prefer foods high in fat and sugar when their appetite was increased. Though these studies were done on animals, we are animals and the facts ring true (Harvard Medical School staff, 2012). Dr. Melanie Greenberg writing in Psychology Today uses the example of a busy mom cramming cookies while shuttling her kids to after school activities or the same mom gobbling a hamburger and fries while sitting in front of her computer desperately trying to finish a work assignment. This need for sugar and fat goes back to our ancient ancestors who really needed the fuel for fighting off predators. However, we don't use those calories when driving the car or pressing keys. Those calories go to fat — and often to belly fat (Greenberg, 2013). This visceral fat is unhealthy as well as unsightly and is one of the reasons for the upsurge in the incidence of Type II diabetes. The National Institute of Health says that 64% of American women are overweight. Of these, 36% are outright obese. Though more men are considered overweight than women, more women fall into the extremely obese category (US Dept.. of Health and Human Services, 2012).

So now, we have a harried woman who is already struggling with completing all her tasks. She is eating to supply the energy to keep going and she is stressed even further when she tries on her jeans from last winter only to find that the cookies are still stored around her waist. This is enough of a downer, but she may also find that she must spend part of her meager paycheck on drugs to control her diabetes. All that comfort food can result in some real discomfort down the line. Food as medication is too readily available and too costly in the end.

Men are more likely to smoke and drink rather than to over-eat. However, women also resort to smoking to handle stress. Of course, that leads to a whole new list of problems. The American Lung Association reports that lung cancer has now surpassed breast cancer as the leading cause of cancer deaths n women. Smoking is directly responsible for 80% of those lung cancer deaths. Women who smoke are nearly 22 times more likely to die from chronic obstructive pulmonary disease. The "dowager's hump" we see in older women is the result of osteoporosis. In the case of "the hump," it is the vertebrae which are affected. In general, osteoporosis results in bones honeycombed with weak spots in multiple areas and ripe for fracture. The bones of smokers lose mass faster, leading to an increased risk of osteoporosis and hip fracture. Yet I see teenage girls smoking everywhere I go. They have been targeted by the tobacco companies with the message that smoking will keep them slim (American Lung Association, 2014).

Women have a harder time when quitting smoking than do men. Federal data reveals how many ex-smokers there are, but the data does not tell us how many times the women tried to quit before they were successful — or they may be an ex-smoker today but smoking again tomorrow. According to an analysis of twelve clinical trials, women had a 25% lower success rate than men. This does not mean that women in general have less willpower than do men. Instead, it means that cigarettes fill certain needs in females that don't exist or don't exist to the same degree in males. Women report that they smoke for help with a negative mood, to manage stress and to suppress appetite and control weight. Though they want to quit and they know that it is bad for their health and, in the long run, for the health of their children, they are prone to relapse as soon as the stressors come up again (Partnership for a tobacco free Maine, 2012).

It is particularly sad that lower income women are more likely to smoke than are women who are better paid. It is likely that smoking is an expression of independence, a statement that "I am an individual and I can do what I like even if it is bad for me." Lower income people who smoke are likely to be loyal to a certain brand as though that brand were a friend. People in lower socio-economic communities are likely to be surrounded by advertising for cigarettes, as anyone who has looked at the windows of convenience stores can see. Pregnant women in these communities are far more likely to smoke during pregnancy than their wealthier counterparts (Partnership for a tobacco free Maine, 2016). Smoking during pregnancy leads to low birth weight, respiratory problems and birth defects. It has been implicated in SIDS (Sudden Infant Death Syndrome).

What is very hard to understand is how these people afford to smoke. I checked the price of a pack of Marlboros at our local convenience store. A pack is $6.10 including tax. A carton containing ten packs is a mind-blowing $57.18. If a woman limits herself to one pack per day, she still goes through about $171.54 a month just for cigarettes and, if she doesn't have the $171 at one time, she will wind up paying $183 for a month's worth of cigarettes one pack at a time! It must stress the smoking woman further to know she has to come up with that money just to ease her craving.

You may be a solidly in the middle class and well educated but, if you are a working woman, you are helping to pay for the health problems of those who are not in your financial league and, as a human being, you should be concerned about what is happening to those people in this country. There is a general decline in life expectancy, particularly among white non-Hispanic middle aged Americans, especially among those with less education. This decline is associated with smoking, not enough exercise and obesity. It has long been known that, in general, richer people outlive those with less, but research by Anne Case and Angus Deaton, published last year, discovered that the life span disparity among the poor and the wealthier in society is growing (Case, Anne and Deaton, Angus, 2015). American men with the top 1% in income live 15 years longer than the poorest 1%. Among women, the difference is 10 years. Ten Years!

It was surprising to me that health care involvement in the way of medication did not make a large difference in the statistics. Instead, according to Dr. Tom Frieden, director of the Centers for Disease Control and Prevention, what improves health in a community is wide access to social, educational and economic opportunity. Geographically, where more money was used for social spending, including campaigns against smoking and poor dietary habits, the poor lived longer.

The study by Case and Deaton showed a rise in drug and alcohol related deaths, more suicides and accidents among the less well off. When questioned, respondents among this group reported being less healthy both physically and mentally (*New York Times* staff, 2016). Dr. Deaton reports that "there is some deeper distress going on among white middle-aged Americans that may continue to propel these mortality rates higher" (Case, Anne and Deaton, Angus, 2015). Did you notice that the word stress is in distress?

From my experience, I believe that wine has become the destressor for our time. It is tasty, and affordable for most of us if we stick to those that are moderately priced, and drinking wine is a socially acceptable practice. While many of us might not feel comfortable consuming a batch of martinis daily, having a couple of glasses of wine seems a small indulgence. Maybe it is; but women are drinking more than they used to. In a study done by the *Journal of Studies on Alcohol*, 80% of women ages 21 to 40 reported that they drink and nearly 63% of the group 21 to 34 report downing five or more alcoholic drinks in a recent single occasion.

Guess the reason that women give for drinking. Yes, they say it relieves stress. Alcohol does the trick. Most women feel more relaxed, more flirtatious and mentally calm when they drink alcohol. It also makes people more sociable. It is far easier to meet a new man, for instance one with whom you've only had e-contact in the past, if you are fortified with a couple of glasses of wine. In an all-female group, women become fast friends in a hurry if they are all relaxed by alcohol (Greenfeld, 2009).

Of course, the problem with alcohol is that we build up a resistance. As time goes on, it takes more booze to produce the same effect. More booze can lead to liver problems, heart disease and to major distress in family and work areas. Many of the women at our DV shelter have or have had drinking problems. Alcohol is the fuel for many of the flare-ups that send a woman and her children to a shelter, hiding out from the man whom she once thought she loved. Many of our clients admit that they drink because "it makes them feel better." It is a form of self-medication with a dosage that must always be increased.

What constitutes drinking too much? The USDA and the US Dept.. of Health put out guidelines every year on what is healthy. Using these guidelines, it is not healthy for a woman to have more than seven drinks per week. So one glass of wine before dinner might be OK but two is too much, at least on a daily basis. What is "a drink," by the way? A standard drink is a 12 oz. beer, 5 oz. of wine or 1.5 oz. of a distilled spirit like gin or whiskey. Remember that 5 oz. is just over half a cup — really small! My quite ordinary wine glasses will hold a full 8 oz. cup when filled to the brim, and there are plenty of larger glasses out there.

And it is a fact that women get drunk faster because they have a lower blood volume, due to their smaller size. We feel the effects sooner. Because of this, women are often over the limit sooner than men. According to one source, a 140-lb. woman can be over the limit after only one drink on an empty stomach (US Health and Human Services, 2015). Not only can drinking lead to legal problems, alcohol also lowers inhibitions. It can't be a good feeling to wake up in some guy's bed, not able to remember whether you took precautions.

I'm sure many women for whom drinking has become a habit started out thinking that it was a choice and they could "quit anytime." Nevertheless, estimates state that nearly five million women in the US are alcohol dependent. Not only are we more likely to drink to alleviate stress, we also drink to allow ourselves to be more convivial, despite the stress we may be feeling.

Women are also just as likely to inherit a tendency to alcoholism as men. A genetic link to addiction has long been established. One of the major downsides to alcoholism in women, in addition to the health hazards shared by both sexes, is that it also increases the risk of osteoporosis; and drinking during pregnancy can lead to fetal alcohol syndrome and other birth defects. The cost of easing your stress with alcohol can be high, indeed.

I think we all know what the medical community's response is to the woman who goes to her doctor complaining of stress, either in depression mode or anxiety. She is handed a prescription for Prozac, Lexapro, Zoloft or a host of others for depression; Xanax, Valium or Ativan if she is anxious. Harvard health reports that 23% of women in their 40s and 50s take antidepressants. Wasn't that the age group we called the sandwich generation? Women are 2 ½ times more likely to take an antidepressant than men. Surprisingly, antidepressant use does not vary with income level. It seems that feeling stressed is for everyone. Harvard says the use of antidepressants has increased by 400% between 1988 and 2008 (Wehrwein, 2011).

There is no doubt that these drugs can help, and in some cases the mental anguish is not caused by stress or some particular life event but is, instead, a fundamental malfunction of brain chemistry. I don't discount or advise against using these drugs if they help you but they all have side effects. Julie Holland, a psychiatrist for twenty years, believes that women are dampening their best assets with the use of these drugs. She feels that it is our natural emotional flexibility that allows us to sense the needs of our babies and of others in our lives. She says that the SSRIs, Selective Serotonin Reuptake Inhibitors, such as Lexapro and Prozac, make it hard to enjoy sex properly and also reduce the ability to cry — which would, in itself, alleviate the stress we may be feeling. She feels that anxiety and tension are a by-product of suppressing our emotions. Yet we suppress them further with mood altering drugs. She calls it "cosmetic psychopharmacology" (Holland, 2015).

Why are people turning to psychopharmacology, especially women? Could it be that they worry more often about possible job loss and also suffer the most by what is now referred to as time compression? The internet defines time compression as a requirement for doing more work in less time. Sound familiar? According to the National Institute of Occupational Safety and Health, in the last twenty years, the average work year for prime age working couples has increased by 700 hours. This couple is obliged to squeeze an extra 17.5 weeks into their working year. There is no doubt that Americans are among the hardest working developed nations in the world. Women, already so busy, watch the ads for drugs on television. The pharmaceutical industry spent $2.5 billion in marketing via direct to consumer advertising (National Conference on State Legislatures, 2013). Imagine a single working woman or a married woman trying to do it all. Taking a pill must seem a reasonable solution.

Having been a working mother for so many years and having worked for demanding and insensitive bosses, I think there are better answers to stress than pills. I think that changes in the way a woman reacts to the duties and responsibilities, which are so often dumped on her by other people, can be just as effective as medications and a lot cheaper. We must not let other people run our lives. They don't have the right to make us sick or worse. Suicides among women have risen sharply. A recent newspaper article gave the increase of suicide among women 45-64 years old to be 43% in the last thirty years. That is almost half again as many suicides among women of that age group now, as opposed to in 1986. Indeed, the suicide rate for the whole country is the highest it has been since that year. Allowing for white women alone in middle age, the increase was an appalling 80%. One study cites social and economic disappointment (*New York Times* staff, 2016). I can understand why a woman of middle years who is alone, burdened with a job that expects much and delivers little, would be depressed. Unfortunately, our society offers little in the way of therapy and social interaction. Instead, we offer pills.

Several of the drugs mentioned above are not recommended for long-term use. In addition to alcohol, the other mainstay of the abused women I meet in our shelter is the prescription drug. We do not allow them to keep their medications in their rooms since the rooms are shared by other women. They are required to keep their prescriptions in their lockers in the office. Since I answer the phone in that office, I see what they take out of that locker and it is amazing. The locker is often full, bottle after bottle, both with prescription meds and with over the counter pharmaceuticals. I am convinced that there must be interactions between those drugs but the patient may not be aware of the conflicts, since she got them from different doctors and different pharmacies. She hangs onto all of them like a lifeline, worried that she won't be able to get her refills, managing her time so as not to miss a single dose. It is a commentary on the lives these women have lived and they are not alone.

Opiate deaths among women increased by a multiple of five from 1999 to 2010. In 1999, the number of women who fatally overdosed was 1,287. By 2010, it was 6,631. According to the

CDC, eighteen women die every day from prescription painkillers. Many of these women started on opiates for a legitimate reason, usually treatment for pain. Dr. David Sack, an addiction specialist with Promises Treatment Center says that people assume, because a doctor prescribed the drug, that the drug is safe. Prescription painkillers like Vicoden (hydrocodone), Percocet (oxycodone) or Fentanyl do not have the dubious reputation of street drugs like cocaine or heroin. Women are medicating for a pain, which in reality is often mental or emotional in origin. Many women who abuse prescription painkillers have been sexually abused or otherwise traumatized. The pain, whether physical or emotional, doesn't end and the need for the drug doesn't, either. We are not talking young girls experimenting with drugs here, though that problem certainly exists. The bulk of the female deaths from opiate painkillers was in the 34–54 age range (Aleccia, 2013).

A relative of mine died from an overdose of oxycodone (Percocet) at the age of 44. He had undergone a shoulder injury and received a prescription which turned out to be the beginning of the end. This was a good and hardworking man who knew he had a problem but few treatment centers are available. President Obama recognizes the dangers from these ubiquitous drugs. After listening to a 3-year-old's mother describe how she became addicted first to prescription drugs, then to heroin, the President proposed $1.1 billion in new funding for drug treatment facilities. There is also a plan to help community treatment centers to expand enough to treat 124,000 new patients. He blames the resurgence of heroin in this country to the prescribing of opiate painkillers, citing the fact that 250 million prescriptions for opioids are written every year, "enough for every person in America to have a bottle of pills and then some (*Washington Post* staff, 2016)." Florida now has a computer network among pharmacies that allows pharmacists to detect the abuse of prescription painkillers if the person presenting the prescription has had the same or a similar drug filled in another pharmacy recently. This has cut down on the people who went from pharmacy to pharmacy having prescriptions filled for narcotics. Since opiate addicts can no longer get their prescriptions filled in this way, some are turning to heroin.

Not drug related, though perhaps just as expensive, we come to Retail Therapy as a way of handling stress. My friend used to have a sampler on the wall espousing, "I owe, I owe, so it's off to work I go." Cute but too true. I know many techs who spend their first day off doing laundry, cleaning and cooking for the week ahead, but the second day they spend at the mall. Of course, it is fun and exciting to buy something new. It's the modern equivalent of hunting and gathering, right? However, it can get out of hand. When it's therapy, you are trying to get over some negative experience or emotion. If you bomb a work assignment or have a fight with your boyfriend, a purchase can be an upper. You put it on the card and it's painless. The good feeling is due to the flood of dopamine, a hormone dubbed the pleasure hormone, that flooded your brain at the moment of purchase. It's a temporary high but the bill at the end of the month can bring on a low (*Self Magazine*, 2011).

The majority of Americans shop for pleasure. There can be positive aspects. Knowing you look good in a new outfit can give you confidence when you are making a presentation. There is the creativity of assembling a "look"; shopping for the right accessories, matching colors and shoes. It gives a sense of accomplishment. Shopping online can be done from home when the kids are in bed, a time just for you. However, when you make the click that purchases, it needs to be an item you can afford, not something that, in the light of day, makes you feel guilty that you splurged on it and stressed that you now have to pay for it.

I find it depressing to be writing this chapter, but it doesn't have to be this way. As a supervisor in the lab, when I was baffled by a dysfunctional procedure, I would ask, "Why are you doing it like this?" The answer was all too often, "Well, that's the way we've always done it." I was very likely to give them the rejoinder, "You know, if you always do what you always did, you'll always get what you always got." Let's do something else.

CHAPTER 15. WHAT CAN WE DO ABOUT THE SITUATION?

Much has already been done. When I talk to my friends who came up with me through the dark times of rampant sexual harassment and pay disparity, we realize that it is definitely better now. At least, if your boss propositions you, or you find that you are making less than a male in a comparable position, there is redress. Business analysts believe that there are signs that women are moving up in the business world. Recent data indicates that having more women in senior positions leads to greater profitability. Companies whose leadership is comprised of at least 30% females had net profit margins up to 6% higher than companies that had fewer women in leadership positions. A local technology company, Tribridge, has evened out its Board of Directors with equal numbers of men and women and reports that it is easier now to hire women with technology skills. This company also offers 12 weeks of paid maternity leave (Trigaux, 2016).

I find another point of light in the results of a survey of women ages 22 to 35, who graduated from college within the last 10 years. According to Ann Friedman of New York magazine, when these women were asked why they left a job, they did not give the tired old answer of "it's time to focus on my family." Instead, they cited a lack of opportunity to learn and develop in the old job or a shortage of meaningful work. The number one reason they gave was, "I found a better paying job elsewhere" (*Washington Post*, 2016). Well paid workers stay around. Finally, we are searching out opportunity and grabbing it as men have always done. The women of this generation can afford to call the shots because they are going to be in demand. The Baby Boomer generation is retiring. The generation of new workers is far fewer in number. It could be an employee's market in the future.

I realize that we are not all between 22 and 35, just starting our careers, and we already have responsibilities to consider beyond a better paying job. Many of us have jobs, houses, kids, husbands and parents. We feel that we are sinking under the weight of it all. Firstly, realize that you can change your personal situation. Caretaking is what we women do and have always done but it doesn't need to be wearing us out. Some suggestions for helping yourself cope are given in *The Hurried Woman Syndrome* (Bost, 2005). The first idea is to simplify; that is, simplify in multiple ways. It is easy to get over committed and often hard to say no but it is imperative that we learn to do so. Mom says she never sees you anymore. Your friends say, "I thought we were going to get together." Your son wants to play soccer now in addition to baseball and your daughter wants to take dance lessons in addition to her other school activities. Husband is moping. Dr. Bost attests that, though individual needs are important, no family member should be expected to sacrifice unreasonably for any other member's individual goal. That concept is one that we, as women, mothers, daughters, friends or wives must remember. We do not owe them our lives and we are doing them no favor if, by doing too much, we teach them to expect more from the world than the world is going to give them in the future. Minister Gregory Johnson co-chair of New York City Caregivers says that he has "buried more caregivers than care recipients" (Sheehy, 2010). Tell hubby, mom, son, daughter or friend that you have to say no to them because you have to take care of yourself right now. It is not a choice. It is a necessity.

Practical suggestions are easy to find though not so easy to do. Remove clutter. It is a fact that, the more "stuff" you have, the harder it is to clean around it and the more disarray it will cause. That disarray will prey on your mind. In addition, you do not need to be doing all the cleaning and decluttering. Husbands and kids can go through closets. Give them a bag to fill and re-mind them that if they aren't using it, it is only sensible as well as charitable to give it to someone who can use it. Alternatively, have a garage sale. They will be encouraged if a little money will come out of it.

Assign jobs. It is so much simpler if everyone knows what they are expected to do. Kids can care for pets. They can fold and put away their own laundry. Husbands can cook meals. So he only knows how to make pasta; eat pasta once a week. If everyone likes it, he'll be encouraged to branch out. On Saturdays, make cleaning the house a group effort. Figure out what needs to be done and assign chores according to age and ability. One thing to remember, however, is that it may not be done the way you would have done it. It almost certainly won't be. Accept it! This is caring for you. Accept the effort and suppress the urge to do it over!

When my children were young, I worked in a clinic. The other tech and I took turns staying late every other month. We both had children and this was a challenge since we seldom got off before 6PM. I learned to have the next night's meal half done. It was tiring the first night, as I had to make that night's dinner as well as get the next one started, but it made a big difference from then on. If I planned a meatloaf, I made the meatloaf and put it in the fridge. I washed and salted the baking potatoes. The next night I could call my son and ask him to put both in the oven about 5:30. When I came home, there was just time to heat frozen vegetables and dinner was done. Even a salad can be made ahead. I then made spaghetti sauce for the next night's meal while the kids cleared the dishes. It freed up our evenings and it was such a blessing to come home to the fragrance of a good meal cooking rather than to starving, whiny kids in addition to a sullen husband.

I do yoga and find it very restful as well as good exercise. Just a few poses have been proven to give confidence and power. The positions that take up space, arms outstretched in a V (for Victory) or hands on hips like Wonder Woman, actually help to increase testosterone, the hormone associated with power, and to reduce cortisol, the stress hormone. We tend to slump when we are tired and worried, to hug ourselves for comfort. Using the power poses along with deep breaths can make you feel better. Even if the situation hasn't actually improved, you will feel more able to deal with it (Dorfman, 2016).

Anyone can breathe properly and do some strengthening moves but you may not have the time for regular practice. What you can do is get outdoors. People need natural light. I found working under fluorescent lights all day sapped my energy. Most laboratories don't even have windows. Of course, you can get too much sunlight, but you don't have to spend all day in the sun to benefit. It is believed that sunlight increases the flow of serotonin. We've already ascertained that a low level of this neurotransmitter can lead to depression. A moderate amount of sunlight helps with bone formation and is even said to discourage some forms of cancer (Nall, 2015). Even without the physical effects, it is good to get outside either by yourself or with your family. My children, now adults, say they remember the small picnics we had as some of our best times together. It doesn't have to be a big production, just some PB&J and drinks shared at the playground or after walking a nature trail. Kids have sharp eyes. They might spot a bird's nest, an animal, or even just a flower. When you become familiar with the trail, you can do scavenger hunts. List a few items that they are likely to see and another few that would be a "find." Let the kids compete as to who gets the most or who sees the items first. You will all be refreshed.

If you don't have children or your children are grown, walk with a spouse or a friend. Tear your thoughts away from your to-do list and teach your eye to spot birds, plants or cloud formations that you never noticed before. I have found solace by just going to the nearest store with a nursery section and looking at the flowers.

The most important advice that I can give you is to ask for what you want. Your husband is not going to figure it out. Your boss is not going to invite your request. We women must take the initiative to ask and to expect delivery. I was raised to put everyone else first. I am 71 years old not and I would still be dead last if I hadn't learned to stand up for myself. This is important in the workplace, but it is even more important at home. Get over the idea that making sure everyone and everything is clean and fed is your responsibility. That may be so when you have babies or toddlers, but it soon becomes the responsibility of everyone living in the house, not just you.

As women, we must never discount the value of our sisters, if not biological then emotional. Women friends are invaluable as a support system. Have a few friends who will listen to your problems even if it is only over the phone. These friends should be people who not will judge you, who will not compete with you. If you have to worry about whether your house is clean when you ask that woman over, she should not be your confidant. Don't share too soon. You will get a feel for the people you work with. If, in time, you find a few co-workers, who do not gossip, do not delight in the discomfiture of others, who seem to be genuinely concerned with your welfare, cultivate their friendship. Invite them to share their concerns with you and be supportive. Sometimes all you can do is listen and sometimes that is all they can do for you but it will certainly help.

Close friends should be the kind who will bolster your self-esteem, not tear it down. I have had a friend for fifty years who came to the rescue of my self-esteem recently. Your grown children espouse beliefs that you do not understand. They may seem disapproving of your opinions. When I felt this way, I said to her that I must have been a bad mother for my child to be so different. She immediately took my part. "You were not a bad mother," she said. "I was there. You were not a bad mother!" That is the kind of friend I am talking about.

Many employers offer their employees psychological help as a benefit, usually called the Employee Assistance Program. The option may only cover a few free sessions with a licensed counselor but take advantage of it. You will feel better if you talk about it and the person to whom you are speaking has no vested interest. They can be impartial. We all have self-doubts. Divorce, rebellious children, problems at work can undermine your ability to make decisions. You may feel that you simply don't know what to do. A counselor will not tell you what your action needs to be, but your options will be easier to see after you talk about your feelings.

I realize that you are busy and that you guard any free time jealously but no woman is an island. You must also involve yourself in the outside world. Get your news from an unbiased source. I recommend BBC America. They have no axe to grind. Change must come if humanity is to meet the challenges of a growing population and growing income disparity. The Global Gender Gap Report for 2009 states it well," A nation's competitiveness depends significantly on whether and how it educates and utilizes its female talent" (Hausman,Ricardo; Tyson, Laura; Zahidi, Saadia, 2009). When I see the economic conditions present in some of the Moslem world, not only do I see the results of never-ending conflict among themselves, I also see that fully half their population is not allowed to contribute beyond cooking meals and bearing and raising children. I'm sure many women in that part of the world are happy with that role but I am also sure that many are not and they have little recourse. Not only would more money come into the household if those women who want to work were allowed to do so, it would also take the burden off the men who are now expected to carry it all, even in a disrupted economy.

We can't all run for public office but you can make up your own mind about the issues and vote! You do have power. You have rights. Use them. Women have been outvoting men for the last 30+ years. Still, only 63.7% of the eligible female voters actually cast a vote in the 2012 election (Rampell, 2014). I hear women say, "Why bother? It doesn't make any difference." Not so. Margaret Mead said, "Never doubt that a small group of thoughtful, committed citizens can change the world; indeed, it's the only thing that ever has." What would have happened if Lilly Ledbetter had given up, or Susan B. Anthony?

It is not only vitally important that we vote in the presidential elections. We must be sure to be represented in Congress, both at the state and national level. Many of the laws that affect women originate there. Cuts in access to health care, birth control or childcare almost always slip by at the state level while we are worrying about how we'll get to work with the car in the shop. Even if you do not depend on government programs to help with expenses, there are long-term injustices that need to be corrected, reference the first chapter on Social Security Spousal Benefits or subsidy reform. Our president, while important, has only limited power. The laws requiring time and a half for overtime, or mandating the Family Medical Leave Act, or the

Pregnancy Act, had to be passed by Congress; and Congress has not been worker- or female-friendly lately. We need more women representing us. Obviously, if we have few female legislators, few family-friendly policies will come to pass.

Income inequality is a fact and it definitely affects you. Corporations are not paying their fair share. Just this year, the president praised the Treasury Dept.. for taking steps to avoid inversion by corporations. Inversion is defined as the practice; more common all the time, of an American corporation buying into a foreign company and then moving its legal headquarters to the home country of the partner, while the American company continues to do business as usual over here. This move allows the corporation to avoid paying taxes in the US and puts more of the tax burden on you, the American Working Woman. Headlined as an example in this effort to force companies to pay American taxes on profits made in America was the proposed merger of American pharmaceutical giant Pfizer with Allergan, an Irish company. The move would have allowed Pfizer to save hundreds of millions of dollars in US taxes by moving its headquarters to Dublin, at least on paper (Associated Press, 2016). Almost certainly due to bad press, the merger did not go through. However, when the hoopla dies down, they may try again. Even though the Treasury Dept.. may discourage the practice, it is still legal until Congress makes it otherwise.

Lest you feel sorry for Pfizer, they make Lipitor and Viagra, both cash cows, and Allergan makes Botox and Restasis. I just filled a prescription for Restasis, eye drops for persistent dry eyes. The cost for 60 tiny vials, one per day, was $446.84 without insurance. Of course, if I buy it in Canada, it will cost only $283.36. Obviously, the American drug manufacturers have a big influence on our government. Our Congress should reign in our corporations in general but it is particularly odious that a company that is making so much money from the health care needs of the American people wants to get out of the taxes it owes on those profits. It is up to you, the American voter, to vote for people who will not make you pay more for a needed drug than your neighbor will in Canada and will not let American corporations escape their responsibilities.

It should be easy to vote. Citizens of Florida are not able to register online, a convenience that would make it easier for young people and busy women to register. However, many states do allow online voter registration and voting can be done by mail if you don't want to go to the polls.

Of course, this is assuming that you have some way of going online. Not all Americans have access. According to a survey done by the Brookings Institute, the American Dream is a pipe-dream. If you are born poor in the USA, you are likely to remain so. And the poor don't vote. Politifact checked a statement by presidential candidate Bernie Sanders, who said that "80% of poor people did not vote." Politifact found the statement to be mostly true. Though efforts have been made to get lower income people registered and to the polls, it has not made an appreciable difference. Political analysts consider the main reason why poor people don't vote to be a simple lack of time (Emery, C. Eugene, Jr. and Qui, Linda, 2016). We have talked about changes that could make it easier for people in general to vote, such as making voting day a holiday and allowing registration on the same day as voting takes place. However, I think we simply must get the word out to poor people that their vote does count. Conditions could be better for Americans in general if changes were made, and voting is a prime way to make change happen.

In the 1950s, there were manufacturing jobs that paid well but required little education. Minimum wage workers in the US in 1965 made about 50% of the average wage of all US workers (Frederickson, 2015). This was before our manufacturing companies either went under due to foreign competition or moved their operations to a country where they could get cheaper labor and/or avoid paying US taxes. Now, there are few jobs for young people that don't require at least high school. Most good jobs require education beyond that. It is no secret that students in poor areas do not get the same education while earning that high school diploma. Because our schools are funded from property taxes, the children of people who pay more taxes get more funding for their schools. The children of the people who rent, though they are paying property taxes indirectly through their landlords, are not represented by name. Their children may be the ones who do not have a computer at home, and they are the

least likely to get one at school. There is a project called Con-
nectAll which aspires to getting 20 million low-income people
on to high-speed internet by 2020. This would not only help students with homework but would also make it possible for more
people to apply for jobs as most applications are now online. It
is known that people who search online get jobs 25% faster than
those without access to that resource. The F.C.C. has proposed
revamping its old phone program to allow wireless and fixed
broadband services to low income housing. If this program is
successful, 82% of homes would have access to the internet as
opposed to the 76% that enjoy that service now (King C., 2016).
We all want to see people working rather than living off welfare. This is a step in that direction and, at least in some states,
the adults could register to vote online, even the minimum wage
mother getting home at 11 PM.

We should also raise the minimum wage. It is a myth that it is
teenagers who hold minimum wage jobs. In fact, the average age
of a minimum-wage worker is thirty-five. Most of these workers
are supporting families. They are not "secondary earners," working for luxuries. Women make up 55% of the total minimum
wage workforce. Almost 20% of the 75 million children in this
country have one parent working for minimum wage, which, at
this time, is $7.25/hr. (Frederickson, 2015). The average hourly
wage in the US today is $21.38 (US Dept.. of Labor, 2016) so ob-
viously, rather than the minimum wage amounting to one half of
the average hourly wage as it did in the 60s, today it is slightly
more than one-third. Some states have their own higher minimum wage laws. Florida does not. As to the argument that raising the minimum wage would hurt teens looking for summer
work, there is a simple work around. Make a special exception
for teens. That is done in Australia and, FYI, the standard minimum wage in Australia is $17.29/hr.

The welfare and subsidy systems need reform. I say that and
I consider myself a liberal, but having generations of people
living off the taxpayer is a surefire way to foster resentments.
The people paying the taxes resent welfare recipients for taking their money and the welfare recipients resent being looked
down on by the taxpayer. People living on welfare do not have
the material possessions that they see on TV or in the homes

of wealthier people. They see no way of ever being able to afford those things and, in truth, they are probably right since, as we said in the previous paragraphs the poor today are likely to remain poor. When a child grows up with time on his hands, resentment in his heart and no hope for anything better, the idea of taking what he wants from someone else is all too likely to occur. Street crime, gangs, teen pregnancy are all symptoms of wanting to be proud of yourself for something, whether it is your new baby, your gang membership or the laptop you stole out of someone else's car. That satisfaction is what most of us get from work. Any work can be a source of pride if you take pride in doing it. However, there needs to be some hope for minimum wage or welfare parents that their children can do better. Their children need to have the education and incentive that could lift them out of poverty and that education and incentive begins long before first grade. Many parents do not know how to teach life skills. They are frustrated and often angry. Their children would benefit by being enrolled in a daycare that could impart social and academic lessons. I personally believe this to be more important than using welfare funds to allow children above the age of two to remain in a home where the mother is trapped and demoralized.

I see nothing wrong with the idea of "workfare" which limits the time a person can draw welfare and encourages them to get paying jobs. However, we cannot expect these people to be able to work if we don't make childcare available. We need childcare centers that are not just for the poor, centers that charge fees on a sliding scale that enables more women to take advantage of subsidized childcare. It makes no sense for one mom who makes $40,180/yr. to get subsidized childcare and another mom who makes $100 more to be excluded from any help and to wind up paying multiple times as much for care. Extending the income limit for what resources are already available is an absolute must but from what I have seen in government-subsidized daycares, there are too many children per teacher to accomplish real learning. Small classes and better-trained teachers would cost more but children graduating from them could start school without being at a disadvantage from the get-go. They would then grow up knowing how important it is to feed young minds when they have children themselves. Mothers of all income levels would be free to establish themselves in jobs if they chose to do so — and to take pride in being able to care for themselves. As a side benefit, women who previously were unable to work because they have children would no longer be in the position of having to stay with an abusive man because, without his help, they can't pay the bills. Affordable childcare that is more than baby sitting is one of our country's greatest needs. If done right, it would pay for itself in less welfare, less crime, lower prison populations and a lot less stress for moms.

Remember the Single bracket racket. It, like the Spousal Social Security benefit, is yet another giveaway to married non-working women (or men). The Single bracket makes you pay more tax on the same amount of money just because you are single, even if you are single with children. It is another archaic law meant to help the family when only the husband worked. The whole unwieldy tax law needs revising but we could start with asking our Congress to make the rate equal on an equal amount of money. Perhaps the married couple with children would pay a higher tax but, if they were getting a break on childcare that they didn't get before, it would even out.

Maybe you don't vote because you don't hear any candidate who talks about these issues. We women have to give them the ideas. Most experts will tell you not to bring up more than one issue when writing to a politician. However, you have limited time. I suggest a laundry list of grievances, suggestions below.

1. The spousal Social Security benefit is unfair to working women. We are doing everything the stay at home spouse is doing but we are not entitled to that benefit if we have paid in ourselves. Either give us what we earn on our own record plus the spousal benefit or eliminate the Spousal benefit altogether.

2. I should not be eligible for less in alimony or in a property settlement, because I have worked. It is unjust for non-working spouses to get more money in a divorce just because they did not work during the marriage.

3. I should be paid equal pay for equal work. The fact that I will have babies is to society's benefit. I should have

paid leave to care for those babies in the first crucial months and I should be able to return to work without censure.

4. Assistance with the cost of childcare is long overdue in this country. What little support the government has offered goes only to the poor and there is an arbitrary cutoff, which discourages me from getting a raise or moving up. Teaching preschools with qualified teachers should be a first priority for government. In 2008 the Joint Economic Committee, the USA congressional body that reviews economic conditions, found that the only families in this country who have seen a real increase in their income are couples in which both parents work. Both of these people pay taxes. They deserve some recompense.

5. Welfare needs reform. The emphasis should be on preparing recipients for paid work in fields where work is available. Their children should be eligible for good childcare that will enable their synthesis into a society that values work and rewards it.

6. Eliminate the Single Tax Bracket. A single taxpayer should not pay more than a married taxpayer on the same amount of income.

7. Our population is aging. Nearly half the people over 80 are expected to get Alzheimer's disease (Alzheimer's Association). Caretakers must have relief. Extend Medicare to cover more nursing care or pay family caretakers to take on that responsibility at home.

8. Our health care system is unjust and unwieldy. There should not be three different prices for the same procedure. There should be one standard price, which everyone pays. Negotiate for better prices with the drug companies. Americans should not pay more than Canadians do for the same medication.

9. Eliminate the sales tax on tampons, sanitary pads and diapers. Those things are necessities, not luxuries.

10. Help the working American woman. Force employers to eliminate split shifts, shifts assigned at the last minute and schedule changes without consultation. These practices take advantage of women who are dependent on their jobs and they need our protection.

Eleanor Roosevelt is quoted as saying, "Do one thing every day that scares you." That is good advice. If you've never sent a letter to your Congressman, do it now. They are supposed to be working for you. If you feel that you deserve a raise, get your reasons together and ask for it with confidence. If you need more help with the cooking, laundry and housework, demand it. If you feel that you are overwhelmed with the primary care of an ailing mom, let it be known. Ask your siblings. Ask her friends. Ask her doctor. You are a working woman, a proud, contributing member of society. Make your voice heard!

BIBLIOGRAPHY

Aeroweb staff. (2015). Retrieved Apr 26, 2016, from Top 100 US Government Contractors: http://www.bga-aeroweb.com/Top-100-US-Government-Contractors-2015.html

Alba, M. (2014, May 9). *VA by the numbers, How big is it and who used it?* Retrieved Mar 19, 2016, from NBC NEWS: http://www.nbcnews.com/storyline/va-hospital-scandal/va-numbers-how-big-it-who-uses-it-n101771

Aleccia, J. (2013, July 2). *NBC News Women's Health*. Retrieved Mar 30, 2016, from Opiate overdose deaths skyrocketed in women, CDC says: http://www.nbcnews.com/health/opiate-overdose-deaths-skyrocketed-women-cdc-finds-6C10509026

AllLaw. (2015). *Legal Info*. Retrieved Feb 13, 2016, from Calculate Child Support Payments in Florida: http://www.alllaw.com/calculators/childsupport/florida

Alzheimer's Association. (2012). *Alzheimer's.org*. Retrieved Aug 11, 2016, from 2012 Alzheimer's Disease Facts and Figures: https://www.alz.org/downloads/facts_figures_2012.pdf

American Lung Association. (2014). *American Lung Association*. Retrieved Mar 26, 2016, from Woman and Tobacco Use: http://www.lung.org/stop-smoking/smoking-facts/women-and-tobacco-use.html?referrer=https://www.google.com/

American Psychological Assoc. (2016). *American Psychological Association*. Retrieved Mar 26, 2016, from Gender and Stress: http://www.apa.org/news/press/releases/stress/2010/gender-stress.aspx

Andrews, T. M. (2016, Apr 26). Millenials booming,baby. *The Washington Post*, pp. 1A,7A.

Associated Press. (2015, June 8). Study: Some for-profit hospitals charging 10 times Medicare rates. *The Tampa Bay Times*.

Associated Press. (2016, Apr 6). Obama lauds effort to curb tax loophole. *The Tampa Bay Times*, p. 4B.

Badger, E. (2014, Jun 23). *The Washington Post*. Retrieved Feb 22, 2016, from The one time America almost got universal child care: https://www.washingtonpost.com/news/wonk/wp/2014/06/23/that-one-time-america-almost-got-universal-child-care/

Barnett, C. (2015). *Rain:A Natural and Cultural History*. New York: Crown Publishers.

Baxandall, Rosalyn and Gordon, Linda. (1995). *America's Working Women, a Documentary History*. New York: W.W. Norton and Company.

Baxter, E. (2015, Apr 14). *Center for American progress*. Retrieved Mar 2, 2016, from How the Gender wage gap differs by occupation: https://www.americanprogress.org/issues/women/news/2015/04/14/110959/how-the-gender-wage-gap-differs-by-occupation/

Baycare. (2015). *St. Joseph's Child Care Center*. Retrieved Nov. 20, 2015, from Tuition Schedule: https://baycare.org/careers/benefits/st-josephs-child-care-center

Belk, D. M. (2012-2016). *The True Cost of Health Care*. Retrieved Mar 16, 2016, from Diagnostic tests: http://truecostofhealthcare.net/diagnostic-tests/

Biography.com (na). *Nancy Pelosi biography*. Retrieved Apr 24, 2016, from Biography.com website: http://www.biography.com/people/nancy-pelosi-38487

Biography.com (na). *Bella Abzug biography*. Retrieved Apr 24, 2016, from Biography.com website: http://www.biography.com/people/bella-abzug-9174815

Biography.com (na). *Biography.com website*. Retrieved May 26, 2016, from Margaret Sangar: http://www.biography.com/people/margaret-sanger-9471186

Bost, B. W. (2005). *The Hurried Woman Syndrome*. New York: McGraw Hill.

Brinegar, B. (2016, Mar 24). *The Huffinton Post BLOG*. Retrieved Mar 2, 2016, from Our Women mean business; Encore careers after 40: http://www.huffingtonpost.com/bobbie-brinegar/our-women-mean-business-e_b_6527110.html

Broome, C. (2015, May). *claudiabroome.com*. Retrieved Feb 13, 2016, from Why Does Divorce have such a Negative Effect on Women?: http://claudiabroome.com/divorce-fact-women-are-the-losers/

Brudnick, I. A. (2014, Dec 30). *Congressional Research Service.* Retrieved Aor 22, 2016, from Congressional Salaries and Allowances: In Brief: http://library.clerk.house.gov/reference-files/114_20150106_Salary.pdf

Buckler, A. C. (1994). *Everything a Working Mother needs to know about Pregnancy Rights, Maternity Leave, and Making her Career Work for Her.* New York: Doubleday.

Burkett, E. (2016). *Encyclopedia Brittanica online.* Retrieved Mar 2, 2016, from The Women's Movement: http://www.britannica.com/print/article/647122

Business Women's Council. (2012). *National Business Women's Council.* Retrieved Mar 3, 2016, from High Growth Women Owned Busness Access to Capital: https://www.nwbc.gov/research/high-growth-women-owned-businesses-access-capital

CAWP. (2016). *Center for American Women and Politics.* Retrieved Mar 13, 2016, from Rutgets, Eagleton Institute of Politics: http://www.cawp.rutgers.edu/current-numbers

CBS. (2015, June 30). *CBS/AP News.* Retrieved Feb 26, 2016, from Obama to expand overtime pay for millions of workers: http://www.cbsnews.com/news/obama-to-update-overtime-pay-threshold/

CCDF, F. (2014-2015). *Child Care and Development Fund (CCDF) Plan.* Retrieved Nov. 2015, from Child Care and Development Fund (CCDF) Plan: http://www.floridaearlylearning.com/sites/www/Uploads/files/Oel%20Resources/2014-2015_CCDF_Plan_%20Optimized.pdf

Center for Disease Control. (2011, Sept 11). *Centers for Disease Control and Prevention.* Retrieved Mar 8, 2016, from Family Caregiving: The Facts: http://www.cdc.gov/aging/caregiving/facts.htm

Center for Medicare and Medicaid Services. (2014, Oct.). *Center for Medicaid and CHIP Services.* Retrieved Jan 30, 2016, from Income Eligibility Stds, Monthly Income, Family size of three: https://www.medicaid.gov/medicaid-chip-program-information/program-information/downloads/medicaid-and-chip-eligibility-levels-table_hhsize3.pdf

Chairman's Blog. (2014, Jan 2). *American Academy of Science.* Retrieved Mar 27, 2016, from Why do women suffer more from depression and stress?: http://www.stress.org/why-do-women-suffer-more-from-depression-and-stress/

Charleswell, C. (2015, Mar 5). *The Hampton Institute.* Retrieved Apr 22, 2016, from Disproportionate Representation: A Look at Women Leadership in Congress: http://www.hamptoninstitution.org/women-in-congress.html#.Vxp3jPkrLZ5

Chatzky, J. (2015, July 14). *Today.* Retrieved Apr 10, 2016, from Pad your pocketbook with file and suspend: http://www.today.com/money/social-security-tips-pad-your-wallet-file-suspend-t31831

Children and Families Administration. (2016, Jan 19). *Office of Community Services.* Retrieved Feb 7, 2016, from Low Income Home Energy Assistance Program: http://www.acf.hhs.gov/programs/ocs/resource/consumer-frquently-asked-questions#Q11

Clark, K. M. (2016, Mar 19). Lawmakers retain after-school funds. *The Tampa Bay Times,* p. 6B.

Clarke, P. (2016, Jan 11). *Legal Match.* Retrieved Feb 13, 2016, from Child Custody Battle between Unmarried Parents: http://www.legalmatch.com/law-library/article/child-custody-between-unmarried-parents.html

Cohen, A. (1996, Vo 6 Number2). *The Future of Children Princeton/ Brookings.* Retrieved Feb 27, 2016, from Financing Childcare: https://www.princeton.edu/futureofchildren/publications/journals/article/index.xml?journalid=56&articleid=326&sectionid=2180

Cohn, D. (2014, April 8). *Pre Research Center.* Retrieved Dec 8, 2015, from 7 key findings about stay at home moms: http://www.pewresearch.org/fact-tank/2014/04/08/7-key-findings-about-stay-at-home-moms/

Confessore, Nicholas; Cohen, Sarah;Yourish, Karen. (2016, Oct 15). *New York Times.* Retrieved Apr 28, 2016, from The Families Funding the 2016 Presidential Election: http://www.nytimes.com/interactive/2015/10/11/us/politics/2016-presidential-election-super-pac-donors.html?_r=0

Cordell, C. (2016). *Resources.* Retrieved Feb 13, 2016, from Florida Child Custody Questions: http://cordellcordell.com/resources/florida/florida-child-custody-questions/

Council of Economic Advisors. (2014, June). *White House office.* Retrieved Feb 27, 2016, from The Economics of Paid and Unpaid Leave: www.whitehouse.gov/sites/default/files/docs/leave_report_final.pdf

Create a Career staff. (2013). *Create a Career.* Retrieved Apr 29, 2016, from The 25 highest paying jobs with only a Bachelor's degree: http://createacareer.org/highest-paying-careers-bachelor-degree/

Das, A. (2016, Mar 31). *Top Female Soccer Players Accuse U.S. Soccer of Wage Discrimination.* Retrieved July 7, 2016, from *The New York Times:* http://www.nytimes.com/interactive/2016/03/31/sports/soccer/us-women-soccer-wage.html

Deaton, A. C. (2015, Sept 17). *Proceedings of the National Academy of Sciences.* Retrieved Apr 13, 2016, from Rising morbidity and mortality among white-non-Hispanic Americans in the 21st century: http://www.pnas.org/content/112/49/15078

Dempsay, Rachel and Williams, Joan C. . (2014). *What Works for Women at Work.* New York: New York University Press.

Dept. of Housing and Urban Development. (2015). *HUD's Public Housing Program.* Retrieved Jan 24, 2016, from Rental Assistance: http://portal. hud.gov/hudportal/HUD?src=/topics/rental_assistance/phprog

DePillis, L. (2015, Feb 24). *Mom's are the real wage-gap victims.* Retrieved October 2015, from Tampa Bay Times, reprint from The Washington Post: http://forums.tampabay.com/opinion/columns/ moms-are-the-real-wage-gap-victims/2218940

Dill, K. (2015, Feb 9). *Forbes Leadership.* Retrieved Apr 29, 2016, from The 20 best paying jobs for women 10 2015: http://www.forbes.com/sites/kathryndill/2015/02/09/ the-20-best-paying-jobs-for-women-in-2015/#584ddcbf36e9

Dorfman, S. (2016, Apr 30). Stressed ot? Strike a power pose. *The Tampa Bay Times,* p. Personal Best 5.

Dreisbach, S. (2010, Oct 10). *NBC News quoting from Glamour.* Retrieved Mar 29, 2016, from Why anxiety disorders among women are on the rise: http://www.nbcnews.com/id/39335628/ns/health-mental_health/t/ why-are-anxiety-disorders-among-women-rise#.Vvrox-IrLZ4

Duke Energy. (2015, Nov.). *Our Residential Rates as of January 2016.* Retrieved January 28, 2016, from Duke Energy, Florida: https://www.duke-energy.com/pdfs/pe-rates-pefresidentialrateinsert.pdf

Dullea, G. (1985, Nov. 7). *The New York Times.* Retrieved Feb 13, 2016, from How Women Fare in no-fault divorce: http://www.nytimes. com/1985/11/07/garden/how-women-fare-in-no-fault-divorce. html?pagewanted=all

Dychtwald, M. (2010). *Influence;How women's Soaring Economic Power will Transform our World for the Better.* New York: Hyperion.

Early Learning Coalition. (2015). *Early education Lifelong success.* Retrieved Feb 11, 2016, from Accreditation: http://www.elcmdm.org/our_services/ accreditation/accreditation.htmlEllis, Renee R. and Simmons,Tavia. (2014, Oct). *US Census Bureau.* Retrieved Mar 8, 2016, from Coresident Grandparents and Their Grandchildren: 2012: ://www.census.gov/ content/dam/Census/library/publications/2014/demo/p20-576.pdf

Emerge America staff. (2016, na na). *Emerge America.* Retrieved May 30, 2016, from Women Leaders for a Democratic future: http://www. emergeamerica.org/home

Emery, C. Eugene Jr. and Qui, Linda. (2016, Apr. 25). Politifact. *The Tampa Bay Times,* pp. 1A,7A.

Evans, B. (2013, May 9). *Daily Mail.com.* Retrieved May 19, 2016, from Bennetton admits it made clothes in illegal Bangladesh factory that collaspsed killing 900 workers: http://www.dailymail.co.uk/news/ article-2321843/Benetton-admits-clothes-illegal-Bangladesh-factory-collapsed-killing-900-workers.html

Florida Dept. of Children and Families. (2015). *Benefits.gov*. Retrieved January 22, 2016, from Florida Food Stamp Assistance: http://www.benefits.gov/benefits/benefit-details/1244

Florida Dept.. of Children and Families. (2012, July). *Temporary Cash Assistance Fact Sheet*. Retrieved Feb 10, 2016, from Automated Community Connection to Economic Self-Sufficiency: https://www.dcf.state.fl.us/programs/access/docs/tcafactsheet.pdf

Florida Dept.. of Children and Families. (2016, Jan). *Temporary Assistance to Needy Families*. Retrieved Apr 14, 2016, from An Overview of Program Requirements: https://www.dcf.state.fl.us/programs/access/docs/TANF%20101%20final.pdf

Florida's Office of Early Learning. (2015, June 1). *ELC of Pasco/Hernando Coalition*. Retrieved Nov. 18, 2015, from Sliding Fee Schedule: http://www.phelc.org/downloads/policy-proced/Sliding%20Fee%20Scale_Pasco_060115.pdf

Francis, R. W. (1998). *The EWqual Rights Amendment*. Retrieved Apr 24, 2016, from The History behind the Equal Rights Amendment: http://www.equalrightsamendment.org/history.htm

Frederickson, C. (2015). *Under the Bus; How Working Women are being Run Over*. New York: The New Press.

Fry, M. (2016, Jan 4). *NJBIZ*. Retrieved Mar 24, 2016, from How women business owners can avoid being overcharged: http://www.njbiz.com/article/20160104/BREAKINGGLASS/160109981/how-women-business-owners-can-avoid-being-overcharged

Fulciniti, F. (2015, July 22). *Prep Scholar*. Retrieved May 30, 2016, from Pell Gant Eligibility and Requirements:Do you Qualify?: http://blog.prepscholar.com/pell-grant-eligibility-and-requirements-do-you-qualify

Fuller, M. (2013). *Working with Bitches*. Philadelphia: DaCapo Press.

Genworth. (2015). *Genworth*. Retrieved Mar 4, 2016, from Cost of Care Survey: https://www.genworth.com/dam/Americas/US/PDFs/Consumer/corporate/130568_040115_gnw.pdf

Gillespie, P. (2014, November). *Part-time jobs put millions in poverty or close to it*. Retrieved October 2015, from CNN Money: http://money.cnn.com/2014/11/20/news/economy/america-part-time-jobs-poverty/

Gleason, J. R. (1991, Oct na). *Monthly Labor Review*. Retrieved May 29, 2016, from Child Care:arrangements and costs: http://www.bls.gov/mlr/1991/10/art2full.pdf

Greenberg, M. (2013, Aug 28). *Psychology Today*. Retrieved Apr 7, 2016, from Why we gain weight when we're stressed and how not to: https://www.psychologytoday.com/blog/the-mindful-self-express/201308/why-we-gain-weight-when-we-re-stressed-and-how-not

Greenfeld, P. (2009, Sept 30). *Women's Health*. Retrieved Mar 29, 2016, from Women and Alcohol: http://www.womenshealthmag.com/life/drinking-too-much

Griffin, J. (2016, May 23). In a time of great change. *The Tampa Bay Times*, p. 4B.

Grossman, J. (1978, June). *US Dept.. of Labor published originally in The Monthly Labor Review*. Retrieved Feb 26, 2016, from Fair Labor Stds. Act of 1938: Fair Labor Standards Act of 1938:

Gwen Graham staff. (2016, Apr 21). *Gwen Graham*. Retrieved Apr 22, 2016, from Meet Gwen Graham: http://gwengraham.com/meet-gwen/

Hartocollis, A. (2016, Mar 10). Berkeley Law School Dean Was Harasser, a Suit Says. *The New York Times*, p. A18.

Harvard Med staff. (2008, July 1). *Harvard Health Publication*. Retrieved Mar 29, 2016, from Anxiety and Physical Illness: http://www.health.harvard.edu/staying-healthy/anxiety_and_physical_illness

Harvard Medical School staff. (2012, Feb 1). *Harvard Medical Publications*. Retrieved Mar 26, 2016, from Why stress causes people to overeat: http://www.health.harvard.edu/newsletter_article/why-stress-causes-people-to-overeat

Hatch, J. (2016, Jan 26). *The Huffington Post*. Retrieved Mar 24, 2016, from Women pay more for dry cleaning because they are women: http://www.huffingtonpost.com/entry/women-pay-more-for-dry-cleaning-because-theyre-women_us_56a66ac4e4b076aadcc769d4

Hausman,Ricardo; Tyson, Laura; Zahidi,Saadia. (2009, na na). *The World Economic Forum*. Retrieved May 27, 2016, from The Global Gender Gap Report: books.google.com/books?id=GkloecRaQc8C&pg=PA24&lpg=PA24&dq=a+nation%27s+competitiveness+depends+significantly+on+whether+and+how+it+educates+and+utilizes+its+female+talent&source=bl&ots=sHVzMsq4lH&sig=uagRlNTWtqhVdhmpwjzLXiCLlwE&hl=en&sa=X&ved=0ahUKEwjD7O

Hellmich, N. (2013, May 1). *USA Today*. Retrieved Jan 30, 2016, from Cost of Feeding a Family of Four: http://www.usatoday.com/story/news/nation/2013/05/01/grocery-costs-for-family/2104165/

Henry Kaiser Family Foundation. (2014). *State Health Facts*. Retrieved Apr 24, 2016, from Population Distribution by Gender: http://kff.org/other/state-indicator/distribution-by-gender/

Hill, C. (2016, Apr 12). *MarketWatch*. Retrieved Apr 26, 2016, from 6 times its more expensive to be a woman: http://www.marketwatch.com/story/5-things-women-pay-more-for-than-men-2014-01-17

Hill, S. (2014, Mar 7). *The Nation*. Retrieved Apr 22, 2016, from Why does the US still have so few women in office?: http://www.thenation.com/article/why-does-us-still-have-so-few-women-office/

History Art and Archives staff. (na). *History, Art and Archives*. Retrieved Apr 28, 2016, from US House of Representatives: http://history.house.gov/People/Listing/W/WOODHOUSE,-Chase-Going-(W000714)/

History.com staff. (2010). *History.com*. Retrieved Mar 1, 2016, from American Women in WWII: http://www.history.com/topics/world-war-ii/american-women-in-world-war-ii

Holland, J. (2015, Mar 6). *CNN*. Retrieved Mar 30, 2016, from Are drugs stifling women?: http://www.cnn.com/2015/03/03/opinion/holland-women-depression-drugs/

Holmes, H. (2015, Jan 16). *7 on your side*. Retrieved Mar 25, 2016, from Woman gets outrageous bill from plumber for simple toilet repair: http://wjla.com/features/7-on-your-side/7-on-your-side-va-woman-gets-outrageous-bill-from-fairfax-plumber-for-simple-toilet-repair-110648

Hoskins, T. (2014, Dec 10). *The Guardian*. Retrieved May 19, 2016, from Luxury Brands: higher standards or just a higher mark-up?: http://www.theguardian.com/sustainable-business/2014/dec/10/luxury-brands-behind-gloss-same-dirt-ethics-production

Human Rights Watch staff. (2011, Feb 23). *US Lack of Paid Leave Harms Workers and Children*. Retrieved Feb 27, 2016, from Weak Laws Discrimination Bad for Families and Business: https://www.hrw.org/news/2011/02/23/us-lack-paid-leave-harms-workers-children

Human Rights Watch staff. (2015, April 22). *Human Rights Watch* . Retrieved May 19, 2016, from Bangladesh: 2 years after Rana Plaza, Workers Denied Rights: https://www.hrw.org/news/2015/04/22/bangladesh-2-years-after-rana-plaza-workers-denied-rights

Huston, K. (2015, Mar 11). *wane.com*. Retrieved Apr 29, 2016, from Vera Bradley CEO reveals reasons for plant closure: http://wane.com/2015/03/11/vera-bradley-ceo-reveals-reasons-for-plant-closure/

Intuit. (2016). *Turbo Tax*. Retrieved Feb 11, 2016, from Calculate your Withholding: https://turbotax.intuit.com/tax-tools/calculators/w4/

IRS. (2014, February). Retrieved November 2015, from Q&A on Employer Shared Responsibility; Provisions under the ACA: https://www.irs.gov/Affordable-Care-Act/Employers/Questions-and-Answers-on-Employer-Shared-Responsibility-Provisions-Under-the-Affordable-Care-Act#Identification

IRS. (2014). Retrieved Nov. 2015, from Child Tax Credit publication 972: https://www.irs.gov/publications/p972/ar02.html

IRS. (2014). Retrieved Nov 2015, from Publication 503: https://www.irs.gov/pub/irs-pdf/p503.pdf

IRS. (2015). Retrieved 2016, from Tax Tables: 2015 Instruction 1040 (Tax Tables) - Internal Revenue Ser

IRS. (2015, June 5). *Small Business and Self Employed* . Retrieved Apr 13, 2016, from Reporting tip income: https://www. irs.gov/Businesses/Small-Businesses-&-Self-Employed/ Reporting-Tip-Income-Restaurant-Tax-Tips

IRS. (2015, Dec. 30). *Topic 751*. Retrieved Jan 30, 2016, from Social Security and Medicare Withholding Rates: http://quickfacts.census.gov/qfd/ states/12/12101.html

Isom, L. L. (2012). *Grace and Grit*. New York: Random House.

Jensen, E. (2009, Nov). *ASCD*. Retrieved Mar 4, 2016, from How Poverty Affects Behavior and Academic Performance: http://www.ascd.org/ publications/books/109074/chapters/How-Poverty-Affects-Behavior-and-Academic-Performance.aspx

Jilani, Z. (2010, Nov 2). *Thinkprogress*. Retrieved Apr 26, 2016, from Three Electoral Reforms that would Improve and Enrich our System of Representative Democracy: http://thinkprogress.org/ politics/2010/11/02/127962/three-electoral-reforms-improve/

Johnson, J. (2002). *Getting by on the Minimum*. New York: Routledge.

Johnston, C. (2015, July 26). Not Just Numbers. *Tampabay Times*, p. 1A and 14A.

Kahn, F. B. (2007). The Gender Pay Gap; Have Women Gone as Far as They Can? *Academy of Management Perspectives, Stanford University*, 7-23.

Kaiser Foundation. (2015). *Kaiser Foundation*. Retrieved Mar 19, 2016, from State Health Facts: http://kff.org/medicare/state-indicator/ total-medicare-beneficiaries/

Kane, J. (2012, Oct 22). *Health Costs: How the US compares with other countries*. Retrieved Mar 16, 2016, from PBS News hour: http://www.pbs.org/newshour/rundown/ health-costs-how-the-us-compares-with-other-countries/

Kaplan, S. (2016, Jan 13). *The Washington Post*. Retrieved Mar 26, 2016, from Female park service emplyees say they were propositioned, groped annd bullied on Grand Canyon river trips: https://www.washington-post.com/news/morning-mix/wp/2016/01/13/female-park-service-employees-say-they-were-propositioned-groped-and-bullied-on-grand-canyon-river-trips/

Kassab, B. (2015, Feb 25). *Child care costs rival college for many*. Retrieved November 2015, from Orlando Sentinel: http://www.orlandosentinel. com/opinion/os-day-care-costs-beth-kassab-20150225-column.html

Katherine Gallagher Robbins, Julie Vogtman and Joan Entmacher. (2014, Sept). *National Women's Law Ctr*. Retrieved Apr 13, 2016, from Minimum wage: http://www.nwlc.org/sites/default/files/pdfs/tipped_minimum_wage_worker_wage_gap.pdf

Kathleen Michon, J. (2016). *NOLO.* Retrieved Apr 6, 2016, from Women buying cars: https://www.nolo.com/legal-encyclopedia/women-buying-cars-30335.html

Keller, E. G. (2012, Nov 9). *The Guardain, US edition.* Retrieved Apr 22, 2016, from Woemn in the US senate: a guide to the 20 female senators: http://www.theguardian.com/world/us-news-blog/2012/nov/09/women-us-senate-senators

Kennedy, L. (2010). *The Daughter Trap.* New York: St. Martin's Press.

King, C. (2016, Mar 10). Obama seeks more affordable broadband. *The New York Times,* p. B2.

King, J. A. (1995). *The Smart Woman's Guide to Interviewing and Salary Negotiation.* Philadelphia: Chelsea House Publishers.

Kittredge, C. (2015, Jan 23). *Women's Health.* Retrieved Mar 25, 2016, from The Physical Side of Stress: http://www.everydayhealth.com/womens-health/physical-side-of-stress.aspx

Klas, A. S. (2016, Apr 21). Another Graham eyes top state job. *The Tampa Bay Times,* pp. 1B,9B.

Kurtz, A. (2013, Jan 13). *CNN Money.* Retrieved Apr 29, 2016, from Why secretary is still the top job for women: http://money.cnn.com/2013/01/31/news/economy/secretary-women-jobs/

Kurtzleben, D. (2013, June 27). *US News and World Report.* Retrieved Mar 24, 2016, from Auto Repair shops really do charge women more sometimes : http://www.usnews.com/news/articles/2013/06/27/study-auto-repair-shops-really-do-charge-women-more-sometimes

Kurtzleben, D. (2015, July 15). *NPR news.* Retrieved 8 2016, March, from http://www.npr.org/sections/itsallpolitics/2015/07/15/422957640/lots-of-other-countries-mandate-paid-leave-why-not-the-us

Leckie, S. (na). *The Labor Site.* Retrieved Mar 1, 2016, from Labor Uinons: http://www.thelaborsite.com/women1.cfm

Lee BK, Glass TA,McAfee MJ,Wand GS,Bandeen-Roche K, Bolla KI, Schwartz BS. (2007, July). *NIH.* Retrieved July 9, 2016, from Association of Salivary Cortisol in Cognitive Function in Baltimore Memory Study: http://www.ncbi.nlm.nih.gov/pubmed/17606815

Lee, J. J. (2013, May 19). *National Geographic.* Retrieved Mar 8, 2016, from 6 Women Scientists Who Were Snubbed Due to Sexism: http://news.nationalgeographic.com/news/2013/13/130519-women-scientists-overlooked-dna-history-science/

Lepore, J. (2014). *The Secret History of Wonder Woman.* New York: Alfred A. Knopf.

Luhby, T. (2014, April 21). *CNN Money.* Retrieved Mar 16, 2016, from Medicare vs. private insurance: which costs less: http://money.cnn.com/2014/04/21/news/economy/medicare-doctors/

Manlove, J. (2010, Jun 10). *Journal of Research on Adolescence Vol. 8 Issue 2 1998.* Retrieved Mar 4, 2016, from The Influrnce of High School Dropout and Social Disengagement on the Risk of School age Pregnancy: http://www.tandfonline.com/doi/abs/10.1207/s15327795jra0802_2

Margenau, T. (2009). *Creators.com.* Retrieved Feb 13, 2016, from Social Security and You: http://www.creators.com/lifestylefeatures/business-and-finance/your-social-security/benefits-to-an-ex-spouse-don-t-impact-current-spouse.html

McCleary, K. (2016, May 17). What People Earn 2016. *Parade,* p. 6.

McCormick, J. L. (2013). *Essential Car Care for Women.* Berkeley: Seal Press.

McGregor, J. (2014, Oct 12). *This CEO's remarks on raises should bother us all.* Retrieved Nov 2015, from Tampa Bay Times: ht

McGregor, Jena. (2014, May 21). *The Washingotn Post.* Retrieved Mar 13, 2016, from Why more women don't run for office: https://www.washingtonpost.com/news/on-leadership/wp/2014/05/21/why-more-women-dont-run-for-office/

McGrory, K. (2016, Mar 18). Florida doctors accept gifts. *The Tampa Bay Times,* p. 7A.

Moon, R. (2014, Jan 9). *Managing Your Church.* Retrieved Apr 26, 2016, from The Pastor Pay Gap: http://www.churchlawandtax.com/blog/2014/january/pastor-pay-gap.html

NAFCC. (2013, fourth edition). *Quality Standards.* Retrieved Feb. 11, 2016, from NAFCC Accreditation: https://www.nafcc.org/file/35a7fee9-1ccf-4557-89d4-973daf84a052

Nall, R. (2015, Nov 9). *Healthline.* Retrieved Apr 9, 2016, from What are the benefits of sunlight?: http://www.healthline.com/health/depression/benefits-sunlight

National Academy of Sciences. (2009, na na). *NCBI.* Retrieved May 29, 2016, from Current Model for Drug Development form Cooncept through Approval: http://www.ncbi.nlm.nih.gov/books/NBK50972/

National Association of Child Care Resources and Referral. (2012, March). *2012 Child Care in the State of Florida.* Retrieved Nov 2015, from NACCRRA: http://naccrrapps.naccrra.org/map/publications/2012/florida_sfs_2012_preliminary_3_20_12.pdf

National Association of Childcare Resource and Referral. (2012, Feb.). *2012 Child Care in the Sate of Florida.* Retrieved Nov. 2015, from naccrra.

National Care Planning Council. (2011, Oct 1). Retrieved Mar 8, 2016, from Can I Get Paid to Care for a Senior Family Member?: http://www.long-termcarelink.net/article-2011-10-10.htm

National Institute for Mental Health. (2016). *Health and education.* Retrieved Mar 27, 2016, from Depression in Women: https://www.nimh.nih.gov/health/publications/depression-in-women/index.shtml

National Institute of Mental Health. (2009, Dec 28). *NIH.* Retrieved July 9, 2016, from Runaway Vigilance Hormone linked to Panic Attacks: http://www.nimh.nih.gov/news/science-news/2009/runaway-vigilance-hormone-linked-to-panic-attacks.shtml

National Women's History Museum. (2007). *Presents: A history of Women in Industry.* Retrieved Mar 1, 2016, from Industrial Revolution 1800-1880: https://www.nwhm.org/online-exhibits/industry/4.htm

National Women's Law Center. (2014). *Stop Discounting Women.* Retrieved Feb 26, 2016, from Underpaid and Overworked; Women in Low Wage Jobs: http://www.nwlc.org/sites/default/files/pdfs/final_nwlc_low-wagereport2014.pdf

NCSL. (2013, Oct). *National Conference os State Legislatures.* Retrieved Mar 30, 2016, from Marketing and Direct to Consumer advertising of pharmaceuticals: http://www.ncsl.org/research/health/marketing-and-advertising-of-pharmaceuticals.aspxNational Conference of State Legislatures

NCSL. (2014, Jan 30). *National Conference of State Legislatures.* Retrieved Feb 13, 2016, from License Restrictions for Failure to Pay Child Support: http://www.ncsl.org/research/human-services/license-restrictions-for-failure-to-pay-child-support.aspx

NCSL. (2016, Feb 4). *National Conference of State Legislatures.* Retrieved Apr 22, 2016, from Women Legislative Leaders: http://www.ncsl.org/legislators-staff/legislators/womens-legislative-network/women-in-state-legislatures-for-2016.aspx

Neighmond, P. (2012, July 13). *NPR.* Retrieved Mar 26, 2016, from Stress, Anxiety, may keep women smoking: http://www.npr.org/templates/story/story.php?storyId=106461484

NFCC staff. (2016). *National Foundation for Credit Counseling.* Retrieved Mar 2, 2016, from NFCC examines history of women and credit: //www.nfcc.org/consumer-tools/consumer-tips/nfcc-examines-history-of-women-and-credit/

Nishizawa, Benkelfat, Young, et al. (1997, May 13). *Differences between males and females in rates of serotonin synthesis in human brain.* Retrieved Mar 26, 2016, from Procedures of the National Academy of Science: http://www.ncbi.nlm.nih.gov/pmc/articles/PMC24674/

Office of the Chief of Information. (2015, July 2). *SECNAV Announces New Maternity Leave Policy.* Retrieved November 2015, from America's Navy: http://www.navy.mil/submit/display.asp?story_id=87987

Paquette, D. (2015, Dec 22). *The Washington Post.* Retrieved Mar 24, 2016, from Why you should always buy the men's version of almost anything: https://www.washingtonpost.com/news/wonk/wp/2015/12/22/women-really-do-pay-more-for-razors-and-almost-everything-else/

Partnership for a tobacco free Maine. (2016). *Partnership for a tobacco free Maine.* Retrieved Mar 26, 2016, from Low income/Education: http://www.tobaccofreemaine.org/channels/special_populations/low_income_and_education.php

Pasco County, F. (2015). *Fares and Pass Info.* Retrieved 2016, from Fare/Fee Type: //www.pascocountyfl.net/index.aspx?NID=1065ndex. aspx?NID=106

Pasco County Utilities. (2014, October). *Pasco County Utilities.* Retrieved January 2016, from Utility Rates: http://www.pascocountyfl.net/ArchiveCenter/ViewFile/Item/2231

Payscale, Human Capital. (2015). *What Am I Worth?* Retrieved Nov. 20, 2015, from Patient care Technician and LPN: http://www.payscale.com/research/US/Job

Payscale, Human Capital. (2016, Jan 12). *Pay Scale.* Retrieved Feb 7, 2016, from Registered Nurse Salary: http://www.payscale.com/research/US/Job=Registered_Nurse_(RN)/Hourly_Rate

Phillips, A. M. (2013, July 19). *Tampa Bay Times.* Retrieved Nov. 20, 2015, from Pinellas forfeits $2.4 million in unspent Child Care money: http://www.tampabay.com/news/localgovernment/pinellas-forfeits-24-million-in-unspent-childcare-money/2132249

Piatt, C. (2014, Mar 27). *on faith.* Retrieved Apr 26, 2016, from 5 reasons why you need a female pastor: http://www.faithstreet.com/onfaith/2014/03/27/5-reasons-you-need-a-female-pastor/31461

Pilon, M. (2015, Feb 13). *The New York Times.* Retrieved Mar 8, 2016, from Monopoly's Inventor: The Progressive Who Didn't Pass Go: http://www.nytimes.com/2015/02/15/business/behind-monopoly-an-inventor-who-didnt-pass-go.html?_r=0

Pinellas County Utilities. (2016, Jan). *Pinellas County Sewer/ Water Utilities.* Retrieved Jan 2016, from Sewer and Water Rates: http://www.pinellascounty.org/utilities/fees.htm#watersewer

Plumer, B. (2013, Feb 28). *How the recession turned middle class jobs into low wage jobs.* Retrieved Feb 23, 2016, from *The Washington Post:* https://www.washingtonpost.com/news/wonk/wp/2013/02/28/how-the-recession-turned-middle-class-jobs-into-low-wage-jobs/

Pomerleau, K. (2015, April 23). *Understanding the Marriage Penalty and Marriage Bonus.* Retrieved Feb 7, 2016, from Key Findings: http://taxfoundation. org/article/understanding-marriage-penalty-and-marriage-bonus

Porter, E. (2016, Feb 28). If you're broke, a nudge won't fix things. *The Tampa Bay Times*, p. 4P.

Porter, L. (2014, Feb 12). *Washington Examiner.* Retrieved Apr 26, 2016, from Defense contractors make three times private sector wages: http://www.washingtonexaminer.com/defense-contractors-make-three-times-private-sector-wages-numbers-show/article/2543940

Post, T. W. (2015, Nov. 13). Women Fall Short with Nest Eggs. *Tampabay Times*, pp. 5 and 6, section B.

Powell, J. R. (2012, July 10). *Today: Rossen Reports.* Retrieved Mar 25, 2016, from Are air conditioning repairers being competent and honest?: http://www.today.com/id/48080346/ns/today-today_news/t/rossen-reports-are-air-conditioning-repairers-being-competent-honest/#. VvWTv-IrLZ4

Press, A. (2016, Mar 26). Grand Canyon Dissolves Unit That Ran Trips. *The Tampa Bay Times*, p. 4A.

Qui, L. (2016, Apr 24). *Politifact.* Retrieved Apr 16, 2016, from Bernie Sanders said Poor People Don't Vote: http://www.politifact.com/truth-o-meter/statements/2016/apr/24/bernie-s/bernie-sanders-said-poor-people-dont-vote/

Rampell, C. (2014, July 17). *The Washington Post.* Retrieved Apr 7, 2016, from Why Women are far more likely to vote than men: https://www.washingtonpost.com/opinions/catherine-rampell-why-women-are-far-more-likely-to-vote-then-men/2014/07/17/b4658192-0de8-11e4-8c9a-923ecc0c7d23_story.html

Ray R, Gornich J, Schmitt J. (2008, Sept). *Parental Leave policies in 21 countries.* Retrieved October 2015, from CEPR Publications: http://www.cepr.net/documents/publications/parental_2008_09.pdf

Realtor.com. (2016, Feb). *Rental units.* Retrieved Feb 2016, from Pasco County: http://www.realtor.com/apartments/Pasco-County_FL?cid=sem_google_desktopdsarentals_cpc_google

Records of Anne Arundel Court. (1703-1765). *Free African Americans.* Retrieved Mar 1, 2016, from Court Records of Anne Arundel Court: http://www.freeafricanamericans.com/AnneArundel.htm

Representation 2020 staff. (na). *Parity perspective.* Retrieved Apr 26, 2016, from Fair Elections: How single member districts hold women back: http://www.representation2020.com/uploads/9/2/2/7/9227685/fair_election_structure.pdf

Reuters. (2014, Dec. 16). *World.* Retrieved Feb 26, 2016, from Wal-mart must pay 188 million in worker's class action: http://www.reuters.com/article/us-walmart-lawsuit-idUSKBN0JU1XJ20141216

Rhodes, M. (2016, Mar 13). Sunday with Sally Field. *Parade,* pp. 8-9.

Rosen, C. L. (2009, Dec). *LegalZoom.* Retrieved Mar 5, 2016, from Men vs. Women: Who Does Better in a Divorce?: https://www.legalzoom.com/articles/men-v-women-who-does-better-in-a-divorce

Saffer, M. (2016, Apr 8). *ESPN W.* Retrieved Apr 13, 2016, from "Dollars but no sense: Golf's long history of shortchanging women", http://espn.go.com/espnw/sports/article/15160220/big-gap- earnings-men-women-professional-golfers

Sanger-Katz, M. (2016, Mar 10). Medicare Tried Experiment to Fight Perverse Incentives. *The New York Times,* p. A17.

Scheiber, N. (2015, July 12). *Growth in the "Gig Economy" fuels work force anxieties.* Retrieved Feb 26, 2016, from *The New York Times:* http://www.nytimes.com/2015/07/13/business/rising-economic-insecurity-tied-to-decades-long-trend-in-employment-practices.html?_r=0

Schrager, A. (2015, Dec 14). *Defense One.* Retrieved May 1, 2016, from How US military structure overcomes the gender pay gap: http://www.defenseone.com/management/2015/12/how-US-military-structure-overcomes-gender-pay-gap/124455/

Self Magazine staff. (2011, May 18). *Flash.* Retrieved Mar 30, 2016, from The Dangers of Retail Therapy: http://www.self.com/flash/fashion-blog/2011/05/the-dangers-of-retail-therapy/

Sheehy, G. (2010). *Passages in Caregiving.* New York: HarperCollins Publishers.

Sherman, A. (2013, Sept. 20). *Tampa Bay Times Politifact.* Retrieved Nov. 17, 2015, from Nan Rich says Florida has long waiting lists for child care...: http://www.politifact.com/florida/statements/2013/sep/20/nan-rich/nan-rich-florida-waiting-lists-child-care-elderly/

Singlemother's Guide, . (2015, May 13). *Temporary Cash Assistance for the Poor.* Retrieved Jan 30, 2016, from TANF: https://singlemotherguide.com/temporary-cash-assistance-for-the-poor/

Smith, A. C. (2016, Mar 6). Women's Issues. *The New York Times,* pp. P1, 5.

Smith, D. E. (2011). *Mom Incorporated; a Guide to Business and Baby.* Portland, ME: Sellars Publishing.

Sneed, T. (2015, March 25). *Supreme Court Rules against UPS in Pregnancy Discrimination Case.* Retrieved Feb 26, 2016, from News: http://www.usnews.com/news/articles/2015/03/25/supreme-court-rules-against-ups-in-pregnancy-discrimination-case

Spencer, N. (2014, Nov 3). *Psychology Today*. Retrieved May 31, 2016, from Why do men sexually assault women?: https://www.psychologytoday.com/blog/insight-therapy/201411/why-do-men-sexually-assault-women

Spinnazi, R; Andreiz, P.; Rossi, G; Nussdorfer, G. (2006, Mar). *Pharmacological Reviews*. Retrieved July 9, 2016, from Orexins if the Regualtion of the Hypothalmic Pituitary-Adrenal axis: http://pharmrev.aspetjournals.org/content/58/1/46.full

SSI, SSDI. (2015). *Social Security SSDI and SSI*. Retrieved Mar 8, 2016, from Supplemental Security Income: https://www.ssa.gov/ssi/text-over-ussi.htm

Statutes of Florida. (2015). *Chapter 61, Dissolution of Marriage; Support; Time Sharing*. Retrieved October 2015, from Florida Statutes and Constitution: Academy of Management Perspectives

Stepp, E. (2015, April 28). *AAA NewsRoom*. Retrieved Feb. 7, 2016, from Annual Cost to Own and Operate A Vehicle : http://newsroom.aaa.com/2015/04/annual-cost-operate-vehicle-falls-8698-finds-aaa/

Taylor, N. F. (2013, Sept 3). *Business News Daily*. Retrieved May 1, 2016, from The Best Jobs for Moms: http://www.businessnewsdaily.com/5032-best-jobs-for-moms.html

The New York Times staff. (2015, Jan 5). Women Short on Options. *TampaBay Times*, p. 4B.

The New York Times staff. (2016, Apr 12). For the poor, geography matters. *The Tampa Bay Times*, pp. 1A,7A.

The New York Times staff. (2016, Apr 22). Suicides rising steeply, study says. *The Tampa Bay Times*, p. 5A

The New York Times staff. (2016, Feb. 29). Arlington bars female WWII pilots. *Tampa Bay Times*, p. 4A.

The New York Times staff. (2016, Apr 21). *Election*. Retrieved Apr 28, 2016, from Which Presidentail Candidates are Winning the Money Race?: http://www.nytimes.com/interactive/2016/us/elections/election-2016-campaign-money-race.html

The Washington Post staff. (2016, Apr 27). Another step in US military history. *The Tampa Bay Times*.

The Washington Post staff. (2016, Apr 30). Gender pay gap affects young hires. *The Tampa Bay Times*, pp. 1B,7B.

The Washington Post staff. (2016, Mar 30). Drug Summitt details misery. *The Tampa Bay Times*, pp. 1A, 6A.

The Washington Post staff. (2016, Mar 27). Well paid workers stay around. *Tampa Bay Times*, p. 5D.

Tisch, C. (2002, Feb 15). *St. Peterrsburg Times online*. Retrieved Mar 25, 2016, from Man faces charges of home repair fraud: http://www.sptimes. com/2002/02/15/NorthPinellas/Man_faces_charges_of_.shtml

Trigaux, R. (2016, Feb 14). Are women set to rise at work? *The Tampa Bay Times*, pp. 1D,2D.

Turner, c. b. (2016, Mar 4). *Deseret News*. Retrieved Mar 24, 2016, from Women may not even realize they are overcharged for these products: http://www.deseretnews.com/article/865649293/Women-may-not-even-realize-they-are-overcharged-for-these-products.html?pg=all

US Dept. of Defense. (2016, Apr 25). *News*. Retrieved Apr 26, 2016, from Contracts: http://www.defense.gov/News/Contracts

US Dept.. of Health and Human Services. (2012, Oct). *National Institute of Diabetes and Digestive and Kidney Diseases*. Retrieved Apr 7, 2016, from Overweight and Obesity Statistics: http://www.niddk.nih.gov/health-information/health-statistics/Pages/overweight-obesity-statistics.aspx

US Dept.. of Health and Human Services. (2015). *2015 Poverty Guidelines*. Retrieved Nov 17, 2015, from Table of Poverty Guidelines: http://aspe. hhs.gov/2015-poverty-guidelines#guidelines

US Dept.. of Labor. (1995, Feb. and March Feb 3 and Mar 30). *Wage and Hour Division*. Retrieved Feb 27, 2016, from FamilyMedical Leave Act: http:// www.dol.gov/whd/regs/compliance/1421.htm

US Dept.. of Labor. (2016, Jan 1). *Wage and hour division*. Retrieved Apr 13, 2016, from Minimum wages for tipped employees: http://www.dol. gov/whd/state/tipped.htm#Florida

US Dept.. of Labor. (2016, Apr 1). *Bureau of Labor Statistics*. Retrieved Apr 8, 2016, from Economic News Release: http://www.bls.gov/news. release/empsit.t19.htm

US Energy Administration. (2015, October 21). *Frequently Asked Questions*. Retrieved January 28, 2016, from How much electricity does the average American home use?: http://www.eia.gov/tools/faqs/faq. cfm?id=97&t=3

US Health and Human Services. (2015). *Nat. Institue for Alcohol Abuse and Alcoholism*. Retrieved Mar 30, 2016, from Women and Drinking: http:// pubs.niaaa.nih.gov/publications/brochurewomen/women.htm

US House Office of the Historian. (2007). *History, Art and Archives*. Retrieved Apr 24, 2016, from Shared Experiences of Women in Congress: http://history.house.gov/Exhibitions-and-Publications/WIC/ Historical-Essays/Introduction/Shared-Experiences/

US News staff. (2016). *US News Careers*. Retrieved Apr 29, 2016, from Job Rankings: http://money.usnews.com/careers

US Small Business Administration. (2016). *US Small Business Administration*. Retrieved Mar 3, 2016, from Office of Women's Business Ownership: https://www.sba.gov/offices/headquarters/wbo

US Social Security Administration. (2015, January). *Benefits Planner, Maximum Taxable Earnings 1937-2015.* Retrieved October 2015, from Social Security Official Website: https://www.socialsecurity.gov/planners/maxtax.html

US Social Security Administration. (2015, May thru present). *RS00615.020 Dual Entitlement Overview.* Retrieved October 2015, from Social Security,Official Website: https://secure.ssa.gov/poms.nsf/lnx/0300615020

US Social Security Administration. (2015, June). *Social Security Press Office.* Retrieved Feb 12, 2016, from Fact Sheet: https://www.ssa.gov/news/press/basicfact.html

US Social Security Administration. (2015, January). *US Social Security.* Retrieved October 2015, from FAQ's What is the maximum Social Security Retirement benefit payable?: faq.ssa.gov/link/portal/34011/34019/Article/3735/What-is-the-maximum-Social-Security-retirement-benefit-payable

US Social Security Administration. (2015, January). *US Social Security.* Retrieved October 2105, from Retirement Planner: Getting Benefits while Working: https://www.socialsecurity.gov/planners/retire/whileworking.html

US Social Security Administration. (2015, January). *2015 Social Security changes.* Retrieved October 2015, from US Social Security: https://www.ssa.gov/news/press/factsheets/colafacts2015.html

US Social Security Administration. (2015, Nov). *Recent Social Security Changes.* Retrieved July 7, 2016, from Social Security: https://www.ssa.gov/planners/retire/claiming.htmlAeroweb staff. (2015). Retrieved Apr 26, 2016, from Top 100 US Government Contractors: http://www.bga-aeroweb.com/Top-100-US-Government-Contractors-2015.html

USDA. (2015, Sept. 30). *Supplemental Nutrition Assisstance Program.* Retrieved Feb 16, 2016, from How much could I recieve: http://www.fns.usda.gov/snap/how-much-could-i-receive

Vera Bradley, I. (2016, Mar 9). *finance.yahoo.com.* Retrieved Apr 29, 2016, from Vera Bradley announces fourth quarter and fiscal year 2016 results: http://finance.yahoo.com/news/vera-bradley-announces-fourth-quarter-130000846.html

Walters, J. (2016, Apr 1). *Newsweek Sports.* Retrieved Apr 13, 2016, from Taking a closer look at the gender pay gap in sports: http://www.newsweek.com/womens-soccer-suit-underscores-sports-gender-pay-gap-443137

Wehrwein, P. (2011, Oct 20). *Harvard Health Publications.* Retrieved Mar 30, 2016, from Astounding increase in antidepressant use by Americans: http://www.health.harvard.edu/blog/astounding-increase-in-antidepressant-use-by-americans-201110203624

Wilmerding, G. (2006). *Smart Women and Small Business.* Hoboken, NJ: John Wiley and sons.

Wojcik, J. (2014, Oct 24). *Women pay more than men for health care benefits.* Retrieved Mar 19, 2016, from Business Insurance: http://www.businessinsurance.com/article/20141024/NEWS03/141029856

Wolf, P. (2015, May 20). *Wolters Klumer.* Retrieved May 18, 2016, from HELP committee chair not happy with EEOC and it's outstanding general counsel: http://www.employmentlawdaily.com/?s=eeoc+backlog

Women, A. A. (2016). *The Simple Truth.* Retrieved Feb 11, 2016, from pdf of report: http://www.aauw.org/files/2016/02/SimpleTruth_Spring2016.pdf

Yglesias, M. (2012, May 14). *Slate Moneybox.* Retrieved Mar 4, 2016, from Why are teen mothers poor?: http://www.slate.com/articles/business/moneybox/2012/05/teen_moms_how_poverty_and_inequality_cause_teens_to_have_babies_not_the_other_way_around_.html

Printed in the United States
By Bookmasters